B7

The
English Landscape
Garden

The
English Landscape
Garden

H.F. Clark

Alan Sutton
1980

Alan Sutton Publishing Limited
17a Brunswick Road
Gloucester GL1 1HG

First published 1948. This edition with
additional illustrations and in larger
format published 1980.

ISBN 0 904387 38 0

British Library Cataloguing in Publication Data

Clark, H Frank
    The English landscape garden. - 2nd ed.
    1. Landscape gardening - England - History
    I. Title
    712'.6'0942   SB477.G7

    ISBN 0-904387-38-0

Printed in Great Britain
by Redwood Burn Limited
Trowbridge & Esher

CONTENTS

PART I

The English Landscape Garden: page 13

PART II

Description of Gardens

THE PLATES

The illustrations marked with an asterisk, although not mentioned in the text, have been inserted as typical of gardens of the period.

1. Claude Lorraine: Sketch for Landscape
2. Claude Lorraine: Sketch for Landscape
3. Claude Lorraine: Study of Trees
4. Holkham Hall, Norfolk
5. *Hare Hall, Essex
6. Hagley Park, Worcestershire
7. *Dalkeith Palace, Scotland
8. Artificial Ruin at Kew Gardens
9. *Ranston, Dorsetshire
10. *Halswell, Somersetshire
11. Kew Gardens: A view of the Wilderness and the Alhambra
12. Kew Gardens: A view of the Palace at Kew from the Lawn
13. *The English Garden at Le Petit Trianon, 1783
14. Blenheim Palace
15. *Unidentified wash drawing by Humphry Repton
16. *Sheffield Place, Sussex
17. *Sheffield Place, Sussex
18. Engraving from drawing by Richard Payne Knight
19. Engraving from drawing by Richard Payne Knight
20. *Barrington, Gloucestershire, 1708
21. *Barrington, Gloucestershire, 1820
22. Chiswick House: Design for the Cascade by William Kent
23. *Designs for Grottoes in various styles from *Détails de Nouveaux Jardins à la mode*, by Le Rouge, Paris, 1776-87
24. Rousham, Oxon
25. Rousham, Oxon
26. Chiswick House and Park: Plan engraved by Le Rocque, 1736

ILLUSTRATIONS IN THE TEXT

FOREWORD

When *The English Landscape Garden* was first published in 1948 not nearly so much interest was shown in landscape gardens. Now there are many garden books of all kinds, but perhaps there is still a place for a book written with so much care and affection for the subject.

I remember well the rather strange circumstances in which it was first conceived. During the war Frank was in the Light Rescue Reserve of Civil Defence, he worked on 24 hour shifts and when he was off duty he spent most of his time at the British Museum writing and researching. I thought this would be the first of many books, but sadly he died about two years before he was due to retire, intending to spend his leisure on a larger work.

I am happy to see this new edition and hope all the people who have been trying to obtain copies will be pleased at its appearance in a new guise and not on war economy paper. Although looking rather different, the text is just as it was in 1948 and it remains Frank Clark's personal statement about the English landscape which he loved so much.

Marjorie Clark
Edinburgh, 1979

PART I

THE ENGLISH LANDSCAPE GARDEN

'IT IS THE peculiar happiness of this age to
see . . . regularity banished, prospects
opened, the country called in, nature rescued
and improved and art decently concealing
herself under her own perfections.'

R. S. CAMBRIDGE *The World* (188) 1755

IT WAS THE FRENCH who first recognized the peculiar English-
ness of that seemingly inconsequential arrangement of shrubs,
lawns and flower beds known as the Landscape Garden. *Le Jardin
Anglais* was a Continental style derived partly from the magnificent
temple-studded landscape park of Stowe and partly from Chambers'
Chinese decorations at Kew. It was an attempt, a poor attempt at
that, to copy the charm which they recognized as existing in 'the
irregular'. From the seventies of the eighteenth century many of the
great French château gardens and some parks, notably those of
Mortefontaine and Ermenonville, were almost wholly landscaped.

The quality of fidelity to nature in the English landscape garden
appealed, of course, to that gentle savage, Rousseau. His immensely
popular novel, *La Nouvelle Héloïse*, published in 1760, established
the fashion for irregularity in France. Rousseau was not only a re-
former but a great descriptive writer of nature. And although he did
not wholly grasp the principles and peculiarities of the English
landscape garden, he should be remembered at least both for his
remarks that a garden walk should be 'somewhat irregular, like the

steps of an indolent man', with which Chesterton's inaccurate but picturesque description of the English Lane is of the same genre, and also for this quotation from his *La Nouvelle Héloïse*. When after a stroll through the garden made by the philanthropic Englishman, Julie says to her lover, 'Well, how does it appear to you . . . are you got to the end of the world yet?' he replied, 'No. I am quite out of the world, and you have in truth transported me into Elysium.' His ecstasy was engendered not so much by the charms of Julie as by the delights of the English garden, Rousseau style, through which he had walked. It was something of this feeling, I suppose, that led the French aristocracy to exchange the formal *allées* of Versailles for those things which the liberty-loving English found so delightful in natural scenery—the cheerful effects of flowery thickets, the sound of singing birds in rustic aviaries, limpid and serpentine rivulets and those elaborate charades and picnics which were the subjects of the picturesque and playful art of the painters, Vernet, Fragonard and Boucher, and the idyllic romance of *Paul et Virginie*.

The word 'Elysium' appears so much in contemporary writing on the English garden that we cannot wholly ascribe it to eighteenth century overstatement. One can find frequent references in the letters of Walpole to such earthly paradises as Kent's 'Elysiums' at Esher and Stowe and in the enthusiastic descriptions of landscape parks by Joseph Heely. It was, of course, a quality of the rarefied air breathed by these eighteenth century connoisseurs, rather than a quality of the landscape itself. It was symptomatic of a state of mind. Looking now at the fragmentary remains of these early gardens it is possible to recapture something of this ecstasy. Their gentle charm is all pervasive. The temples, Classic, Gothic and Chinese, which stand enfolded by trees at the end of green vistas, the winding lakes, too natural to be nature, the mouldering ivy-clad ruins, the manor-house standing on its austere grass platform are the real stuff of that idyllic dream. So it is therefore with a first shock of surprise that we

14

examine contemporary prints of some of the scenes described with such rapture by Walpole and Heely (Plate 36). The whole landscape seems bare and puny, the serpentine streams are devoid of charm, naked and unclothed by planting, the plantations are plantations of saplings, the lawns, rough meadow grass. Their landscape was, it seems, a dream landscape.

A long time ago, a Chinese poet, by the name of Chang Ch'ao, magically anticipated all this in the following epigram: 'There are landscapes on earth, landscapes in painting, landscapes in dreams and landscapes in one's breast. The beauty of landscapes on earth lies in depth and irregularity of outline; the beauty of landscapes in painting lies in the freedom and luxuriousness of the brush and ink; the beauty of landscapes in dreams lies in their strangely changing views; and the beauty of landscapes in one's breast lies in the fact that everything is in its proper place.'

The achievement of the eighteenth century landscape gardeners was just in this quality of rightness. Everything was in its proper place. The landscape was a composition, obeying the rules of the painters, the arching trees framing the view, tree clumps balancing buildings, an irregular sheet of water reflecting the golden evening light, and the foreground enlivened by a flock of grazing sheep or a herd of deer. It is a familiar scene repeated time after time in the canvases of the picturesque landscape painters, from the great masters of the Italian school, Claude and Poussin, to our own Constable. And for the curious, the scene contains the clue to the whole matter: for this landscape was not a construction, mathematically composed in terms of the golden rule, it was animated by a dream, the beauty of which lay in its strangely changing views. Herein lies the quality of strangeness to be found in these gardens. From Claude English gardeners inherited the quest of an ideal, as well as the associations which were so important for their appreciation. Claude was a product of the Italian Renaissance and the Italians were the first among modern peoples to feel, and to transcribe into an art form, their love of nature. Their discovery of the joys of scenery strengthened by strong classical influences resulted in what Mr. Christopher Hussey, author of *The Picturesque*, has termed 'the invention of Ideal Landscape' where nature, constantly struggling to realize her own perfections, had, at last, through the painters' vision, achieved 'form', ' . . . Claude selected and compounded aspects that were calm and idyllic (Plate 1), Salvator those that accentuated the wilderness and fierceness of nature (Page 5). In neither case was it intended to represent nature as she was but as she might have been . . . ' The constant talk of 'improvement' and 'capability' with which conversation of eighteenth century men of taste flavoured their discussions of gardening is indicative of this.

Like the Italians, the English had never been unaware of the beauty of 'landscapes on earth' which Chang Ch'ao attributed to 'depth and irregularity of outline' and which Addison called 'the amiable simplicity of unadorned nature'. Bacon's 'sweet and sightly' wilderness of sweetbriars and honeysuckle and Milton's description of Paradise were examples of our constant affection for irregularity and naturalness. On the foundations of this sensibility towards nature, this realization of what the Chinese poet called 'depth', the painters and poets in the reigns of the Georges were able to create 'Elysiums' more substantial than a dream, full of strangely changing views.

From this appreciation of the beauty of nature came the desire to copy these subtle effects in gardens. For by the reign of Queen Anne, gardens had become over-stiff, clipped and formal and 'unnatural'. Nature herself had less obvious charms to display to those with an eye trained to see them, trained by the study of pictures, and with a memory of the gardens seen on the Grand Tour in Italy and France and the unexampled natural scenery of the Swiss Alps.

A Genoels inv. Romæ

Salvator Rosa: Trees and Hermit

THE STORY OF THE INVENTION of what is known as the landscape garden can only be told in ways as serpentine as Hogarth's line of beauty. The path twists and turns and doubles back on its tracks. For the first experiments, the so-called 'irregular' gardens of the first quarter of the century, are superficially as formal as Le Nôtre's pomp and ceremony at Versailles; and, in the last quarter of the period, when formality was once again permitted, the fashion for the picturesque was at its height.

The path at first is a maze, for it starts in the wilderness. The wilderness to the English means a wood adjoining a garden where what William Robinson contemptuously used to call the housemaid-gardener has not attempted to use the tools of his trade. The paths are grass tracks, curving where necessary round the boles of large oaks or beeches, avoiding the marshy verges of the stream and ending much where they started at the edge of the lawn. The sweet and sightly wilderness, with 'the ground set with violets, strawberries and the like low flowers', was first enclosed in the seventeenth century within the protecting walls of the garden, after it had long been seen and coveted from the medieval green mount. The story of the green mount has little to do with the eighteenth century land-scape except for the conjecture that we must long have shared this symbolic mountain with the traditional lake and island garden of the Chinese, in which the 'Holy Mountain of a myriad beatitudes' stands reflected in the 'Eastern Sea of eternal sunrise'.

The view from the green mount was followed at the end of the seventeenth century by the invasion of the wilderness when the Baroque garden of parade and fashion had pushed out its radiating avenues of trees almost to the horizon. This was the solution of the French, led by Le Nôtre, who extended the dominance of art over nature uncompromisingly and without quarter. But we who had for a century appreciated the sweetness of the natural wilderness approached the problem more obliquely and less logically. The first

18

step was the destruction of the garden wall and the invention of the 'ha-ha', or the invisible wall.

The English gardener realized that his art must be in some sense subordinated to nature and that his designs must include the natural forms found outside his garden walls. The ha-ha, the sunk fence, brought him face to face with something more than a natural wilderness—a Universe. Within the infinite variety and apparent chaos to be found in nature, he had recently been taught to find uniformity and order. For the new scientific discoveries had revealed harmony in the courses of the sun and stars and proportion in the structures of organisms. There is 'Idea of Sense, Order and Proportion everywhere . . . ', wrote Shaftesbury.

And the whole weight of a new philosophical system, in which the work of nature was opposed to the work of the mind, caused him to associate all that was best within the laws of nature, which became sacrosanct, and to despise all that was acquired, artificial or conventional. For the creation of this eighteenth century landscape garden occurred during the slow change from classical rationalism to romanticism. The Romantic movement was the awakening of sensation, of curiosity and the quickening of the mind's eye, the imagination. The Romantic movement originated in England and the landscape garden, a truly romantic conception, was the fruit of its first experiments.

The gardener, therefore, contemplating the wilderness on the other side of the ha-ha, was enabled to unravel nature's apparent disorder, and perceive with imaginative faith, 'nature's genuine order'. But this was not all. Simple nature was the wilderness, the fields and hedges, and if 'nature unadorned' was the model then we would have progressed little beyond the introduction of wildernesses into the garden enclosure, and the Chinese poet's 'landscapes in dreams' would not have materialized. Something more was needed to create those 'strangely changing views'.

19

The path we are following through the wilderness now breaks through the dappled green light of the wood and emerges on to a rough highway that winds through the strange country of France, over the roof of Europe and down into the sunny plains of Italy. On this rough track are the coaches of the eighteenth century 'men of taste', taking the Grand Tour. In them you would find the 3rd Earl of Shaftesbury, Joseph Addison the essayist, the young Lord Burlington and his protégé, William Kent, Horace Walpole and the poet Gray, and, as the century progressed and as the Tour became more and more a fashionable educational institution, a long procession of English gentry, youthful connoisseurs and painters in search of the picturesque. Each of these would be writing their impressions in their diaries or in long and detailed letters to be sent home by courier. The conversation of these early travellers would at first be stilled by the strangeness of the scenery they witnessed. The Swiss Alps would overawe, and the Italian *campagna* be without significance until they had reached the Eternal City. From there the track would double back on the return journey, only now the conversation would be voluble and what had been a tiresome, strange adventure, dusty and dangerous, would assume a new significance. For at last they could recognize the *pittoresque* quality of the countryside and appreciate views and scenery and see beauty and sublimity where before had only been awe-inspiring strangeness. What they had been taught in Rome was to see nature through the eyes of the classical Italian landscape school of painters, Claude Lorraine, Nicolo and Gaspar Poussin, Salvator Rosa, and to recognize those qualities selected for emphasis by these painters when met with in natural scenery. Their *Baedeker* would almost certainly have been Jonathan Richards' *Account of the Statues and Bas-Reliefs, Drawings and Pictures in Italy, France, etc.: with Remarks* (1722). Amongst these remarks were, of course, clear and decisive opinions on the masters they should notice, Claude, Poussin and

Rosa being starred, as well as hints on connoisseurship such as '. . . A connoisseur . . . sees beauties in pictures and drawings which to common eyes are invisible; he learns by these to see such in nature, in the exquisite forms and colours, the fine effects of lights, shadows and reflections, which in her are always to be found . . . and which none with untaught eyes can possibly discern.'

After the romantic landscape of Northern Italy, the return of these travellers to their English seats, to the stiff, rather pompous gardens imported by the Dutchman, William of Orange, to the clipped *allées*, the gravelled parterres and goose-foot avenues made by Le Nôtre's pupils at many great English houses (Plate 20), stirred them to protest. 'English gardens are not so entertaining,' wrote Addison, 'to the fancy as those in France and Italy.' 'Our British gardeners,' he complained, 'instead of humouring nature, love to deviate from it as much as possible. Our trees rise in cones, globes and pyramids. We see the marks of the scissors on every plant and bush. I do not know whether I am singular in my opinions, but for my part I would rather look upon a tree in all its luxuriancy and diffusion of boughs and branches than when it is thus cut and trimmed into a mathematical figure . . .' And to reinforce his unorthodox views, he requoted Sir William Temple's famous remarks, written in 1685, when his readers had been reminded that a great nation (the Chinese) had evolved a system of gardening based on 'artificial rudeness'. By the fifties, fashionable London was to be only too well aware of the Chinese taste, but in Addison's day Chinese Sharawadgi was a useful argument on behalf of change from the regularity of the Dutch and French styles to the new 'irregularity'.

This astonishing word 'Sharawadgi' first startled English eyes in Temple's *Garden of Epicurus*. And though it might well have done so it never won popularity even in a period in which picturesqueness, connoisseurship and chiaro-obscuro, were in common usage among 'men of taste'. The word was used to define a particular

21

type of beauty, which, wrote Temple, 'shall be great and strike the eye . . . without any order or disposition of parts, that shall be commonly or easily observed'. The Chinese affirmed, he wrote, that any child could plant trees in a straight line and at regular intervals but that a high degree of sensibility was necessary to achieve beauty in 'figures' which were not immediately discernible.

Chinese Sharawadgi was therefore useful ammunition in arguments against geometrical design in gardens. It did not, on the other hand, provide experimenters with a ready-made alternative. It was obvious to all that 'a tree in all its luxuriancy and diffusion of boughs and branches' would make nonsense of a pleached *allée* (Plate 3). If nature was to be 'humoured' then a new system, other than one based on the laws and proportions of 'art', had to be found.

All the various impulses which I have mentioned and others which will be described were combined in the creation of the Irregular garden, which with the impetus of its own logic was to develop into the Landscape Park. The new system was to satisfy the English not only aesthetically but also politically. Dr. Pevsner, in an article in *The Architectural Review*, 'The Genesis of The Picturesque', makes this interesting point very clearly. It can be summarized briefly.

When in 1711 Shaftesbury wrote that 'the horrid graces of the wilderness represent nature better and are more engaging than the formal mockery of princely gardens', he was expressing not only the characteristic love of naturalism we have noticed before, but another strong impulse which has been called a conscious anti-French policy in the arts and which manifested itself with the return of the Whigs to power. Le Nôtre's gardens came to symbolize autocracy and the absolute rule of man over nature, the English irregular gardens, constitutionalism and man's alliance with nature. It was partly for this reason that both Rousseau and Montesquieu in France praised the

22

English garden. As the century progressed and as the differences between constitutional monarchy and Continental autocracy became more irreconcilable, both Horace Walpole and Burke and other writers commented on this link between the English Constitution and 'the happy effect of following nature'. Our taste was formed, as Walpole wrote, 'by trade and not by military and conquering spirit...'

THE GARDENER, left during this long digression into first causes still contemplating the ha-ha and musing on the intricacy and mystery of nature, now took the next step which was violent and unexpected. Our gardener was no other than the young William Kent, architect and painter. Horace Walpole has best described what happened. 'The sunk fence ascertained the specific design; and when nature was taken into the plan, under improvement, every step that was made pointed out new beauties and inspired new ideas. At that moment appeared Kent, painter enough to taste the charms of landscape, bold and opinionative enough to dare and to dictate, and born with genius to strike out a great system from the twilight of imperfect essays. He leaped the fence and found all nature was a garden. . . . Thus the pencil of his imagination bestowed all the arts of landscape on the scenes he handled. The great principles on which he worked were perspective, and light and shade. . . .'

Thus William Kent's athletic feat brought him the fame due to any explorer of new worlds. There is no doubt that he was the first to make landscapes using the principles of painting, and to use new forms based on direct observation of nature. His use of water, woods and meadows made the landscape style manageable and they directly resulted in some of the masterpieces of the period, the best preserved of which is Rousham (Plates 24, 25), Oxon. Beside Chiswick, the gardens of old Carlton House, before its conversion into a palace by Henry Holland, were attributed to him, as were Esher Park, Clare-

23

mont, and the gardens of Holkham. The sketch of part of this garden reproduced in this volume (Plate 4) shows clearly enough where Capability Brown learned his famous clump technique. Hagley (Plate 6), Envil and Pains Hill, though not due to him, probably reflect his influence. Walpole's estimate of his capabilities was just. 'He was a painter, an architect and the father of modern gardening. In the first character he was below mediocrity; in the second, he was the restorer of the science; in the last, an original and the inventor of an art that realizes painting and improves nature. Mahomet imagined an Elysium, but Kent created many.'

So the English irregular garden emerged after 'the twilight of imperfect essays' from the pencil of William Kent, though Sir John Vanbrugh's gardens at Castle Howard, Blenheim and Stowe, in collaboration with Charles Bridgman, were only thus described as imperfect by a succeeding generation that had not realized that his picturesque and romantic gardens were in advance and not behind his time.

The success of Kent's 'great system' was due, partly, to two not unimportant factors—its moral integrity and its classical derivations. It was thought to be no mere coincidence that the extravagance and licentiousness of the court of Louis XIV should have taken place among bronze fountains cast to look like trees, trees clipped to imitate stone and parterres embroidered like a petticoat. A cascade or a serpentine stream were considered more honest in their purposes than 'a jet of foetid and muddy water drawn up at enormous expense from a frog marsh'. Such was the opinion not only of Englishmen but also of such Frenchmen as Pierre Daniel Huit. The taste for the irregular was as moral as was rustic life itself and as innocent as the pastoral delights of Virgil's *Georgics*.

The triumph of the irregular occurred during the rise of Palladianism in architecture. Both were derived from classical sources filtered through the work of Italian Renaissance scholarship. The

24

aims of these two arts, gardening and architecture, appear con-
tradictory if the mistake is made in confusing later developments of
the romantic landscape school with the work of Kent. Irregular
gardens were as classical and correct as the buildings of the Burlington group. They were, as Sir Henry Wootton had remarked, 'a
state of contrariety' between buildings and their surroundings, 'for
as fabrics should be regular, so gardens should be irregular'. This
was a truth which classical authority was found to have practised.
The discovery by Robert Castel, Burlington's architect, that classical
Roman villa gardens contained examples which he could describe as
'a close imitation of nature, where though the parts are disposed
with the greatest art, the irregularity was still preserved . . .'
became a strong argument in favour of the new style. Gardeners,
such as Stephen Switzer, claimed that theirs was 'the method laid
down by Virgil in his second *Georgic*'. Addison, whose vogue as a
leader of taste was enormous, brought the weight of his authority to
the side of change by claiming that his own taste was Pindaric, that
in his garden it was difficult to distinguish between the garden and
the wilderness.

Most men of taste in fact soon came to the conclusion, voiced by
one Batty Langley, an architect of the day, that there was 'nothing
more shocking than a stiff regular garden' and proceeded to practise
the new enthusiasm for 'irregular regularities'.

The first of the new irregular gardens was probably Chiswick
Park, which was begun, after Burlington's first visit to Italy, a few
years before 1717, when a temple called 'the first essay of his lord-
ship's happy invention' was reproduced in Colin Campbell's edition
of *Vitruvius Britannicus*. Before this, the work had very possibly
been carried out under the critical eye of Pope and the great contemporary gardener Charles Bridgman. Bridgman and his partner
Eyre were the royal gardeners who are credited by Walpole as the
inventors of the 'ha-ha'.

It was at Chiswick where Kent's first experiments with the new forms were made. The reproductions of his original sketches for parts of the garden (Plates 22, 27) are evidence enough to support Walpole's enthusiastic admiration.

The ground plans of these early rococo gardens showed little alteration from the seventeenth century formal layout. If they were not symmetrical they were still at least formed along strong axial vistas (Plate 26). Pope's garden at Twickenham, which was a model for his contemporaries, contained many of the elements of the formal garden, except where his paths 'twisted, twirled, rhymed and harmonized' in true rococo playfulness.

Pope's influence on his contemporaries was wide. He was the friend and adviser of both Charles Bridgman and William Kent. He was often consulted by his friends on the improvement of their gardens. The rules, which he expounded in his *Moral Essays*, particularly in his *Letter to Burlington*, were accepted as the ultimate authority up to the end of the century:

> 'He gains all points who pleasingly confounds
> Surprises, varies, and conceals the bounds.'

Surprise, variety and concealment became the three prerequisites of the art of landscape.

As has been said, the formality of these Irregular gardens was their most notable feature. And this in spite of the fervent protestations of their creators that nature was their only inspiration. The imitation of nature, however, meant for Kent, Batty Langley, Switzer, Bridgman, primarily a respect for the 'genius of the place' and, lastly, irregularity. Variety produced asymmetrical balances and arrangement and an avoidance of the cardinal sin of the sort of monotony which Pope satirized. 'Grove nods at Grove, each Alley has a brother, and half the platform just reflects the other.' Respect for the genius of the place meant respect for its natural character.

The imposition of a geometrical plan on an irregular site resulted in lost opportunities and often, as Langley lamented, in 'the loss of many Fine Views'. It was at this period that the quest for prospects was begun with such ardour. Here is a description of Esher Park, a garden laid out for Henry Pelham by William Kent, who started work on it about 1729. 'It is built in the form of an old college, and stands in a valley, surrounded by those grounds which are so much and so justly celebrated: they are neither park, garden, nor wood, but a lovely mixture of all three. On the highest eminence stands an octagon summer-house, commanding, from each of its eight windows, a prospect so rich, so various, and so unbounded, that the gazer's eye is oppressed by the profusion of beauties and knows not where to fix. If it be possible to describe, or do justice to this enchanting spot, it must be in the words of that sweetly descriptive poet Thomson.'

Thomson, of course, found the right words, for the poets were the first artists to be influenced by the picturesque. In *The Seasons* Thomson described the scene at Esher with visual imagery as carefully composed as any of Claude's landscapes,

> 'Heav'ns what a goodly prospect spreads around,
> Of hills, and dales, and woods, and lawns, and spires!
> And glittering towns, and gilded streams, till all
> The stretching landskip into smoke decays.'

Henceforward gardens were to be judged as worthy of the connoisseur's attention if the prospects were pleasing, and if it happened to be 'an Albano landskip', a reflection of that vision of nature seen by Claude among the Alban Hills a century before, then, like Horace Walpole, he would 'wear out his feet with climbing, his eyes with gazing, and his tongue and vocabulary with commending'.

One not so fortunate as to possess a commanding site could nevertheless 'make a pretty landskip of his own possessions', by making frequent plantations that 'may turn as much to the profit as

27

the pleasure of the owner'. This was the advice of Joseph Addison, who also reminded his readers that 'fields of corn make a pleasant prospect'. The results of this advice were the *fermes ornées* that were popular in the first quarter of the century, the most famous examples of which were Philip Southcote's Woburn Farm (Plate 36), 'Southcote's Paradise', and The Leasowes of William Shenstone.

So the quest for 'prospect, animated prospect', and the art of arranging natural materials to the forms of painting, using trees to frame the view, teaching 'the gentle stream to serpentine', using nature's undulating line, planting clumps of trees as screens, emphasis or punctuation, and 'comprehending the beauties of light, shade and buildings as a painter would do', became the mission of all men of taste.

The search for prospect and the attainment of Pope's three conditions, 'surprise, variety and concealment', inevitably led the eighteenth century gardener by devious and serpentine ways from the irregular to the picturesque. Kent's rococo style was not followed after his death in 1748. The *fermes ornées* of Philip Southcote, Charles Hamilton and William Shenstone contained motifs which later were to be familiar characteristics of the great landscape parks. The playful, twisting and rhyming paths of Bridgman's and Kent's wildernesses became first a rough field path encircling the estate and finally the road down which Doctor Syntax, mounted on poor Grizzle, was later to ride on his search of The Picturesque through the mountains and lakes of Cumberland and Westmorland.

NOT ALL THE CONNOISSEURS of those days, of course, agreed with the new taste. There were sceptics. In the fifties, Sir William Chambers, with his imagination filled with Chinese 'conceits', as his enemies put it, took a jaundiced view of it all. In his *Dissertation on Oriental Gardening* he wrote: 'Our gardens differ little from

common fields so closely is vulgar nature copied in most of them . . .
these compositions rather appear the offspring of chance than design,
and a stranger is often at a loss to know whether he be walking in a
common meadow or in a pleasure ground, made and kept at a considerable expense . . .' Chambers asserted that nature was incapable
of pleasing without the assistance of art, obviously strongly disagreeing with Walpole that 'the modern gardener exerts his talents
to conceal his art', and William Shenstone's reflection that 'art
should never be allowed to set foot in the province of nature other-
wise than clandestinely and by night'. Also what Chambers never
understood, or had forgotten, was that inner eye which turned those
common meadows into the Elysian fields. The eighteenth century
was an age which believed that it was the association of ideas set up
by an object or a view which produced the beautiful effect and not the
object itself. The imagination was stimulated to conceive a connected
train of thought in sympathy with that first suggested by particular
forms, so that these forms could be called beautiful for having
been the parent of such ideas. Garden scenes were made not only
to please the eye but also to excite the imagination and produce
sensations of grandeur, melancholy, gaiety and sublimity. 'You
must know, sir,' wrote Addison, 'that . . . a garden . . . is naturally
apt to fill the mind with calmness and tranquillity and suggests
numerous subjects for meditation . . .' This was another reason for
variety, for calmness and tranquillity alone would be dull. All kinds
of objects were used to stimulate emotions. Urns and obelisks were
memorials and therefore a stimulus to melancholy, streams were gay
and lively, still pools conducive to quiet meditation, and open views
terminating in classic temples were associated with the golden
harmonies of Claude. These were only some of the evocative symbols
used. Every opportunity was taken to encourage that new romantic
indulgence in feeling for which it seemed eighteenth century man had
a strange craving, though the taste for melancholy is probably a

29

national characteristic. Burton's *Anatomy of Melancholy*, Young's *Night Thoughts*, and Keats' *Ode to Melancholy* appear to suggest that it was present in every century. At any rate, 'in the very temple of delight, veiled melancholy had her sovran shrine . . .' For Kent himself had recorded that he was so overcome by this emotion while sitting under the obelisk at Chiswick that he remained all night, as if enchanted, in that spot until released by the morning sun.

A winding garden path was used to conduct the visitor from one object to the other and to ensure that the effects were viewed in the intended order. The seats were placed at vantage points as punctuation marks to enable connoisseurs to recover breath and balance during their switchback ride from the heights of the sublime to the valleys of gentle arcadian felicity.

Such scenes were arranged in succession, so that variety and contrast were achieved in the transition from one part of the garden to another. Lord Kames described in his *Elements of Criticism* that the purpose of fine art was to stimulate emotion and went on to say that 'in gardening the emotions raised by that art are best so faint, that every artifice should be employed to give them their utmost vigour; a field may be laid out in grand, sweet, gay, neat, wild, melancholy scenes, and when these are viewed in succession, grandeur ought to be contrasted with neatness, regularity with wildness, and gaiety with melancholy'. In fact, Lord Kames felt so strongly the truth of this theory that he was led to believe in its converse. Just as the sight of ornamented grounds promoted benevolence and humanity, so, he asserted, 'rough uncultivated ground, dismal to the eye, inspires peevishness and discontent: may not this be one cause of the harsh manners of savages?'

Water was of course an essential element of the picturesque scene. No painter's landscape would be conceivable without a lake, reflecting in its depths the pastoral Claudian scene. The famous lake at Stourhead, with its circle of temples, is the best known example.

And the torrent and cascade were essential if the romantic wildness of Salvator Rosa was to be successfully reproduced. The roar and rage of a torrent, its force, violence, and impetuosity tended to inspire terror and astonishment, that mixture of feelings which the eighteenth century writers had identified as sublimity.

The very nature of the art of landscape gardening tended to stimulate and encourage sensibility. For what in fact the gardeners were trying to do was not only to satisfy an inherent love of natural forms for their own sake and to reproduce Claudian landscapes but also to recapture the emotions experienced during the Grand Tour when, after leaving the sunny plains of France and Italy, they had ascended the Alps to the very roof of Europe. Suspended between earth and sky they had seen with fearful fascination the complex pattern of the earth at their feet. Mountains, roaring cascades, the evidences of the convulsive forces of nature in these vast ranges, filled them with sensations of awe which they never afterwards forgot. The painter who had best been able to translate this experience into the idiom of paint was Salvator Rosa. Rosa, or Savage Rosa, as he was called, round whose life scandalous legends of lawlessness had become encrusted, the outlaw and friend of those banditti who had threatened their safety in the mountains, became the romantic hero, the pre-Byronic hero, of the age. His canvases, peopled with hermits and banditti and filled with twisted trees, tumbled rocks, cliffs, ruins and racing skies, enabled the traveller to re-experience the delightful horror of such scenery and to appreciate its significance when met with in poetry, the paintings of other artists and in landscape. The correct associational link was made by Walpole in a letter during his tour with Gray in 1739: 'Precipices, mountains, torrents, wolves, rumblings, Salvator Rosa!'

The well-known attachment of the eighteenth century man of taste to ruins was derived from the same source. The massive tumbled arches and colonnades of Rome were a heady draught for

31

the romantic traveller. Jacob Burckhardt, in *The Civilization of the Renaissance in Italy* (1860), recently published in a popular edition, reminds us that these ruins awakened even in the minds of the Renaissance scholars not only archaeological zeal and patriotic enthusiasm but an elegiac and sentimental melancholy. They became a subject for painters even before the births of Salvator Rosa and the great Battista Piranesi. At first, used as backgrounds in paintings of the birth of Christ, this rich mine of association and symbolism was worked by a succession of imaginative painters up to Hubert Robert, *Robert des Ruines*. That ruins should become an essential part of landscape gardening was only logical. As well as invoking melancholy musings on the all-mouldering hand of time, they were also associated curiously enough with an anarchic passion for freedom, which, as Ruskin was later to complain, carried 'the love of liberty even to licence, and the love of wilderness even to ruin, (taking) pleasure at last in every aspect of age and desolation which emancipates the objects of nature from the government of men'.

Ruins had indeed such a strong romantic significance, that, if real ruins were not conveniently to be found on one's estate, the architect, Sanderson Miller, was employed to 'build' them. He is known to have been commissioned by such connoisseurs as the great William Pitt, Chancellor Hardwicke and Lord Lyttleton. It also might be added that the picture of ruined classic temples found in Claude's compositions, their half-buried columns almost engulfed in foliage, taught designers a lesson in the true relationship between art and nature, the column of masonry, the column of the tree trunk, so that the classic ruin was also dearly loved as a decorative motive in other arts, notably those of tapestry and ceramics. Paul Sanders' tapestries for the Duke of Northumberland at Albury Park and the fine blue printed dishes of Wedgwood are examples.

The last and not the least attractive decoration and evocative aid devised was the garden temple. These buildings, either in ruins or complete, became the most natural element in a landscape composition and as necessary and proper to it as the irregular lake and the clumps of trees, half concealing, half framing, the prospect beyond. These garden pavilions were, of course, the descendants of the Palace of Pleasure of Oriental gardens, and the ancestor of our present sun-traps or rustic summer-houses. From the time when the vogue for Claude's pictures stimulated Englishmen into feeling visual pleasure in natural scenes, these small temples became the focal point in the picture. And it was Claude, who, having used the ruins of classic temples in his dreamlike landscapes, firmly fixed the association in the minds of eighteenth century connoisseurs of these temples with the pastoral pleasures of classical Greece. Eighteenth century pavilions dedicated to love and friendship were in this tradition. Most architects during the Georgian period designed these light-hearted and elegant structures. And those of them that remain, like the slender Temple of Eolus at Kew, crowning its daffodil-starred hill, and Burlington's domed, pleasant 'happy invention' at Chiswick (Frontispiece), still retain the power of quickening our interest and pleasure. One of the first was Sir John Vanbrugh's Doric Temple at Castle Howard. This with Hawkesmore's immense mausoleum and other architectural decorations together formed what Walpole described as 'the grandest scene of real magnificence I ever saw'. It was a triumph which Vanbrugh was to repeat at Stowe where he contributed the Rotunda and the Boycott pavilions to 'that fine landscape of Albano', and to which William Kent added his temples, columns and statues, triumphal arches and bridges, and the more ephemeral Dido's Cave, Witch House, and Cold Bath, which have long since vanished (Plate 47). Kent indeed was a prolific designer of garden temples. Less elaborate than Vanbrugh's and all from the same Vitruvian mould, they are more in scale with the landscape and were perhaps more suitable than Vanbrugh's magnificent buildings at Castle Howard and Blenheim. Gothic, of course, made its early appearance as an architectural style for garden temples and an example which can still be seen is the Gothic tent on the crest of a hill at Pains Hill, Cobham (Plate 38). It was built from a design by Batty Langley. Walpole called it an 'unmeaning edifice' and wrote unfairly, considering his own edifice at Strawberry Hill, that 'the Goths never built summer-houses or temples in the garden'. However, in spite of this, the style became fashionable and Gothic ruins and even Gothic grottoes were used to provide that element of variety considered so essential in the picturesque composition.

And to enrich this variety the vogue for Chinoiserie invaded the garden as well as the boudoir. Walpole mentions, with the same feelings of distaste, a Chinese temple at Wroxton in 1753, believed to have been one of the first and to have been erected from a design of one of the brothers Halfpenny. It was, however, William Chambers' buildings at Kew which really stimulated the taste for things Chinese. The great Pagoda (Plate 11) is too well known to need description. His most charming effort, however, was a small 'Ting' pavilion in the old Menagerie which has since disappeared. As shown in a contemporary engraving it appeared to be a light-hearted, decorative piece of confectionery.

The story of the further development of the English Garden can now be told. The poet-painter gardeners had worked out the main principles of the design. The topography of the ground was first studied to see what possibilities there were, what was the inherent pattern of the landscape. The painter's eye was to be used in grouping trees and plants, so that a picture could be composed emphasizing this natural pattern. Then the poet followed, placing his evocative symbols, the temple, the serpentine stream and lake, the ruin, the seats and urns, and connecting them all, the winding path. The early transition gardens, which I have called 'Irregular', were the first experiments. The landscape gardens of the poet-painters followed. These can be conveniently classified as the

34

Landscape Parks, phase one. These were the creations of the landed proprietor himself, 'the proprietors of taste'.

SINCE LANDSCAPE GARDENING was a new type of gardening, breaking away apparently from the traditional forms of the previous centuries, it is not surprising that the chief exponents of this novelty and those best able to carry the stage a step further from the irregular should have been men who had some knowledge of pictures, who had made the Grand Tour and had a knowledge of classical literature. Bathurst, Pope, Burlington, Cobham, Pelham, were the leaders in a fashion which gentlemen of landed property felt it incumbent on them to follow. 'Every man now,' said an essayist in 1739, 'be his fortune what it will, is to be doing something at his Place, as the fashionable phrase is, and you hardly meet with anybody who, after the first compliments, does not inform you that he is in mortar and moving of Earth, the modest terms for Building and Gardening. One large Room, a serpentine River, and a Wood are become the absolute Necessaries of Life, without which a Gentleman of the Smallest Fortune thinks he makes no Figure in his Country.'

Best known of the gardens which became a Mecca for all men of taste to visit were those of Charles Hamilton at Pains Hill, Sir Henry Englefield at White Knights, Southcote at Woburn Farm, Chertsey, William Shenstone at The Leasowes, Lord Lyttleton at Hagley, and the Earl of Stamford's park at Envil.

Two of these, Woburn Farm and The Leasowes, were ornamented farms and have been mentioned. Sir Charles Englefield selected, with singular taste, so Walpole wrote, 'that chief beauty of all gardens, prospect and fortunate points of view'. Charles Hamilton at Pains Hill worked more deliberately than others from Pope's dictum 'that all gardening is landscape painting'. The pictorial effects that he achieved can still be seen, for it is one of the few of these early gardens which were comparatively untouched by Victorian improvers. Hamilton also designed for his friend, the Marquis of Lansdowne, a cascade after a picture by Gaspar Poussin at Bowood (Plate 55). These were the first experiments in attempting wholly visual effects almost undiluted by any other considerations, even those of association. Shenstone's *ferme ornée* at The Leasowes, on the other hand, achieved much of its fame by its pastoral scenes, the appreciation of which was largely literary, while the gardens at Envil and Hagley were a successful mixture of both visual and literary motifs.

It was from these first landscape parks that the landscape forms, which were to become characteristic of the style, were evolved. The books of theory which issued from the pens of writers on gardens from the seventies onwards, such as George Mason, Thomas Whately, William Marshall, and the poet William Mason, acknowledged the quality of the work of these 'amateurs'. The publication, in 1765, after his death, of an essay by William Shenstone, called *Unconnected Thoughts on Gardening*, became as important an event to gardeners as the publication of Pope's *Letter to Burlington*. They are a series of aphorisms which contained all that was most valuable in the ideas of landscape gardening. His subject was almost wholly the pictorial treatment of landscape. He took for granted that his readers would be as familiar as he was with the 'theories of agreeable sensations' as propounded by such writers on aesthetics as Burke, Hutchinson, Gerard, and would agree that 'gardening consists in pleasing the imagination'. Dullness was now the enemy and not regularity. His weapon was 'variety', and 'that variety which the natural country supplies everywhere'. This virtue could only be achieved, he contended, by the methods employed by painters and the use of forms which would constantly keep the imagination stimulated and alert.

To do this Shenstone advised, as might be expected, the use of ruins, which 'afford that pleasing melancholy which proceeds from

a reflection on decayed magnificence', and the stimulation of historical association, if the house and grounds had happened to be the scene
of any event in history. 'Mottoes should allude to it, columns etc.
record it, verses moralize upon it; curiosity receive its share of
pleasure.' Hence, of course, those columns and obelisks which rise
above the trees in all landscape parks, recording the fame of members
of the family or commemorating the visits of the great.

Though by this time it had become axiomatic, Shenstone was the
first to write 'The landscape painter is the gardener's best designer',
and much of the interest in this essay of Shenstone's was contained in
a series of maxims on the use of the eye, which can hardly be improved upon: 'The eye should always look down upon water;
customary nature makes this requisite'; 'The foot should never
travel by the same path which the eye has travelled over before';
'The eye must be easy before it can be pleased'; 'I think a plain space
near the eye gives it a kind of liberty it loves; and then the picture,
whether you chuse it grand or beautiful, should be held up at its
proper distance'; 'The eye requires a sort of balance . . . but not so
as to encroach on probable nature. A wood, or hill, may balance a
house or obelisk.'

It can be gathered therefore, that the natural landscape park
was not a matter of chance—or picturesque neglect as later theorists
were to suggest. Nature left to itself would produce chaos. But
nature assisted by art, its inherent and potential pattern selected
and clarified with a painter's eye, was the ideal to be aimed at. As
has been mentioned, what shocked the eighteenth century gardeners
in the formal garden was the imposition and repetition of artificial
patterns on a site which had its own natural character. It was not
symmetry which was objected to; Shenstone himself advocated a
kind of balance in landscape, but the symmetry of identical masses.
'Apparent art in its proper province is almost as important as
apparent nature,' he wrote, 'but their province ever should be kept

distinct.' The shape of the ground, the site of the trees, the fall of water was nature's province. Buildings, urns, obelisks and other works were art's province. But when, as Shenstone warned them, gardeners begin to compromise, then 'Night, Gothicism, confusion and absolute chaos are come again'.

THE SECOND PHASE of the Landscape Park was dominated by the man whose name is best known to the public and whose gardens symbolize for them the English Landscape Park. Lancelot Brown, better known as 'Capability' Brown, was the first and is the best known professional landscape gardener.

He was a bluff, hearty man with a flippant but persuasive tongue. He was apparently no respecter of persons. 'Mr Brown's flippancy diverted one,' wrote Walpole in a letter to the Countess of Ossory, 'the first peer that experiences it laughs to conceal his being angry at the freedom: the next flatters him for fear of being treated as familiarly; and ten more bear it because it is so like Brown.'

This flippancy of his did not reduce his persuasiveness, for their lordships invariably allowed him to 'improve' their grounds. There is no reckoning the amount of parks he did improve. His popularity and practice were enormous. Walpole related that he refused an invitation to visit Ireland on the plea that he had not yet finished England. And Owen Cambridge, the essayist, is said to have remarked in a conversation with him, that he hoped he would die before him as he would like to see heaven before he had improved it.

He was born in Kirkharle in Northumberland in 1715. He was first a kitchen gardener at Stowe in 1750. His first work as a designer was to make an artificial lake for the Duke of Grafton at Wakefield Lodge, Northamptonshire, in 1764. He afterwards became Royal gardener at Hampton Court. There is a legend that he planted the famous vine there in 1769.

His most successful work was the landscaping of the park at Blenheim (Plate 14). By damming the River Glyme, he widened and enlarged the lake. The effect so pleased him that he happily exclaimed, 'The Thames will never forgive me for this.' It was a feature which he subsequently tried the loyalty of his admirers by repeating too often. And so that the scenery should be as natural as possible and 'no disgusting display of art' might be visible, he tucked away, in surrounding groves, the kitchen garden and flower gardens.

Brown's style is easily recognizable. His fault lay in endless repetition of a formula, the most obvious features of which were circular clumps of trees, the boundary ride or belt, serpentine rivers and his undulating lawns brought up to the very walls of the house. He was, as Mr. Hussey calls him, 'that most dangerous phenomenon, a practical man inspired by a theory. But a theory, moreover, that although derived from visual qualities had become intellectual and standardized.' Mr. Hussey quotes, in *The Picturesque*, an account by Hannah More in which Brown explained his method. During the 'very agreeable two hours' that he spent with her . . . 'he promised to give me taste by inoculation. I am sure he has a very charming one, and he illustrates everything he says about gardening with some literary or grammatical allusion. He told me he compared his art to literary composition. Now there, said he, pointing his finger, I make a comma, and there, pointing to another part (where an interruption is desirable to break the view) a parenthesis—now a full stop, and then begin another subject.'

The trouble was that he never did begin another subject. The next paragraph was a repetition of the first. Parodying this literary simile an unkind critic remarked that 'these big improved places were like sheets of green paper with a parcel of round clumps

39

scattered over them like so many spots of ink flicked at random out of a pen'.

Brown derived the forms he used from the experiments of his predecessors. His visual training he derived from a study of Hamilton, his belt from Southcote's *ferme ornée*, his clumps from Kent and Shenstone. He owed the aesthetic justification of his methods to Burke and Hogarth. 'A Rotund form, in presenting no checks to the eye, simulates infinity,' wrote Burke on the Sublime, 'whether in a building or in a plantation of trees, the Rotund has a noble effect.' 'To distance a building,' said Shenstone, 'plant as near as you can to it two or three circles of different coloured greens . . .' Brown's clumps may have simulated distance to infinity—but the effect was not sublimity.

Whatever quarrel one may have with Brown's methods and style, he was, by the very extent of his practice, almost solely responsible for what Walpole called 'the rapid progress of this happy enthusiasm' which resulted in the humanized English landscape. Landowners whose parks adjoined co-operated in their improvements until large stretches of English countryside reflected that vision of nature seen a century before by Claude. 'How rich, how gay, how picturesque the face of the countryside. The demolition of walls laying open each improvement, every journey is made through a succession of pictures; and even where taste is wanting in the spot improved, the general view is embellished by variety. If no lapse to barbarism, formality and seclusion is made, what landscapes will dignify every quarter of our island, when the daily plantations that are making have attained venerable maturity.' So wrote Walpole, who had watched and championed the new art from its first tentative beginnings. And now that venerable maturity has been reached in the few survivors of Brown's parks, and now that those famous clumps have been thinned and the serpentine streams overhung with trees, one can whole-heartedly applaud his achievements.

Brown died in 1783, a wealthy man, a High Sheriff of London, a man whom Walpole called 'The Monarch of Landscape'. 'Your dryads must go into black gloves, madam,' he wrote to the Countess of Upper Ossory, 'their father-in-law, Lady Nature's second husband, is dead.'

THOUGH IT IS TRUE to say that Brown was the major influence on landscape design from the sixties to the eighties of the century, interesting and ingenious contributions were made by William Chambers, architect to George III and designer of Somerset House and Albany. Chambers' chief criticism of Brown's landscape garden was that it failed to entertain or amuse. He therefore suggested a fresh course of inspiration and, in defiance of the classical traditions, proposed that gardeners should turn to the romantic East. His two books, *Designs of Chinese Buildings, etc.* . . . . (1757) and *A Dissertation on Oriental Gardening* (1772), and the example of his garden at Kew introduced some heresies which both shocked and amused the connoisseurs of the day. The Oriental motifs introduced by Chambers were simply an excuse to exploit the bizarre and grotesque, in the search for novelty. The landscape gardener could and did make use of Palladian, Greek, Gothic and even Turkish buildings, so that a Chinese Pagoda or Temple was only one more attempt to surprise and excite the jaded sense of the men of taste. It was, of course, all very reprehensible, and it was no doubt an example of what Pope would have called 'taste not under the guidance of good sense' degenerating into 'whimsical conceits and absurd anomalies'. He would have been as shocked as was Walpole at Chambers' 'unmeaning falballas of Chinese chequer work'. The joke was, of course, that Chambers' apparently authoritative descriptions of Chinese taste in gardening was a pure invention. The Chinese as a rule were more interested in vegetable gardening. But the decorations and ideas propagated by Chambers resulted in a style which had an immense vogue on the Continent and became known as the *Jardin Anglo-Chinois* (Plate 13).

The most interesting ideas of Chambers', however, were those on planting. They were unfortunately completely disregarded and his theories were only to be rediscovered a century and a quarter later by Gertrude Jekyll and the modern colour planners. 'The Chinese', explained Chambers in his book on Chinese gardening, 'do not scatter their flowers indiscriminately about the borders but dispose them with great circumspection; and, if I may be allowed the expression, paint their way very artfully along the skirts of the plantations . . . they avoid all sudden transitions, both with regard to dimensions and colour; rising gradually from the smallest flowers to the holli-oaks, paeonies, sunflowers, carnations, poppies and others of the boldest growth; and vary their fruits by easy gradations from white, straw colour, purple and incarnate, to the deepest blues and most brilliant crimsons and scarlets.' Chambers also advised that flowers such as larkspurs and mallows, double poppies and loopins (*sic*) should be blended to compose rich, harmonious masses. These ideas were far in advance of his time. Problems of colour were not considered worth serious study by leading eighteenth century landscape gardeners who were concerned only with chiaroscuro, the use of light and shade, and who worked only in tones of green. Shenstone at The Leasowes planted only the simplest meadow flowers which were valued chiefly for their fragrance. Mason in his long didactic poem, *The English Garden*, mentions only a few shrubs, particularly praising the laurel, 'swift shall she spread her broad-leaved shade, and float it fair, and wide'—a wish which, unfortunately, became only too true—and the box, privet, pyracanthus, lilacs, and syringa.

And yet by 1785 William Marshall had published his *Planting and Ornamental Gardening*, which listed about two hundred and seventy trees and shrubs suitable for gardens, including our indi-

42

genous trees, and the catalogue of the plants at Kew, the *Hortus Kewensis*, published in 1789, numbered about six thousand species. Amateur botanists and plant collectors abroad had also begun to send their treasures home. From South Africa had come the asters, Aster novi-belgii and novae-angliae, the parents of the modern Michaelmas daisies, the geranium, later to clothe Victorian lawns in scarlet, and the red-hot poker, Kniphofia aloides; from the Americas the ceanothus, the Phlox paniculata, parent of the modern herbaceous varieties, Magnolia grandiflora, and kalmias, had been added to the garden; and from China, plant collectors had sent back camellias, winter sweet, Chimonanthus fragrans, Magnolia conspicua or yulan and Chinese chrysanthemums. By 1763 the common Rhododendron ponticum had arrived from Spain and a few years later had begun its purple invasion of our shrubberies. So some of the material, at least, was there for the gardener's use.

The chief reason for the lack of colour in the eighteenth century landscape garden is, paradoxically enough, because of the strong influence of painting. The painters of the day, the picturesque school of Gainsborough, Morland and Wilson, were concerned principally with surfaces, picturesque roughness, or with problems of light. Until Constable introduced his revolutionary ideas, Claudian golds and browns were the only proper colours for a picturesque painter to use, since darkness was associated with sublimity. It was when the influence of painting on gardening became less at the end of the century and in early and mid-Victorian times that colour returned to the garden. When it did so, it was unrestrained until French impressionism exerted its influence on Miss Jekyll and her followers.

THE DEATH OF BROWN precipitated arguments as to whether the influence of painting was good or not and whether gardens should be designed in imitation of painters' landscapes. Brown's successor,

43

the new 'Monarch of Landscape', Humphrey Repton, argued for independence, his opponents, Richard Payne Knight and Sir Uvedale Price, for picturesqueness and subservience to painting. The question was also complicated by disagreement on the nature of the picturesque. And now that Brown was dead, criticism of his methods became frequent and shrill. His gardens were described as 'void of genius, taste and propriety' and 'dull and vapid'; he was variously called 'an egregious mannerist', 'a mechanical professor', and 'a snail that crawls all over the ground and leaves his cursed slime wherever he goes'. This last pleasantry was, of course, directed against his love of the serpentine. Brown's chief critics were Knight and Price. Both these men united in their dislike of what they called 'The Brunonian system' though disagreeing on alternatives. Both were landed proprietors and connoisseurs. Knight is better known as a collector of coins, one of the founders of the British Museum, and a writer on Taste, while Price had established himself as an authority on The Picturesque. Although this word had been in current use by con-noisseurs for some years it only really became popular when after 1782 picturesque travel became the fashion and the Rev. William Gilpin published his first descriptive tour of the English counties. Previously it had been concerned with beauty and the imagination or, in other words, a state of mind. The word, as Gilpin used it, then became associated with the appreciation of some visual quality in an object particularly suitable for painting. Generations of British water-colour painters have made these familiar. The qualities thought to be picturesque were chiefly roughness, grotesqueness, varied surfaces, and the objects displaying these qualities were tree trunks, crumbling river banks, gipsy encampments, rough ruins, rocky promontories and mountain crags. Gilpin, for instance, could not admire the Thames at Twickenham, for, in spite of 'its beauty and even grandeur . . . it still falls short, in a picturesque light, of a Scottish river with its rough accompaniments'.

44

The cult of Salvator Rosa and sublimity had thus developed a new category which was thought somehow to be different. Objects were afterwards classified as either beautiful, sublime or grand, or picturesque. The picturesque became the prevailing mode. While travellers and lovers of scenery were visiting the mountains and lakes of Cumberland and Westmorland, the River Wye and the Highlands of Scotland with Gilpin's *Observations* in one hand and sketchbooks in the other, the gardeners were arguing about the relative merits of the beautiful and the picturesque and the two systems which now found themselves in opposition. Brown's 'shaven lawns', green slopes and rounded clumps, the softness of his landscapes, called by Price 'that false beauty of Mr. Brown's', did not accord with the abruptness and rudeness of the picturesque. It was considered unpaintable and therefore unfashionable. Price and Knight wished to found a new school of picturesque gardening. They naturally supposed that the most fashionable practitioner of the day would put their ideas into practice with enthusiasm. They were disappointed.

In one of his letters to Price, Repton wrote that he found, after mature consideration and practical experience, that painting and gardening 'were not sister arts, but rather congenial natures brought together like man and wife . . . and you should recollect the danger of interfering in their occasional differences, and especially how you advise them both to wear the same article of dress'. Repton's attitude grieved Knight and Price. It resulted in a long didactic poem by Knight, called *The Landscape*, which was an attack on Brown and Chambers, and in Price's *Essay on the Picturesque*, and culminated in a series of 'open' letters between the three of them. It was a polite discussion carried on with great urbanity by both sides. The argument can be said to have chiefly centred on whether utility or picturesque effect should have precedence. Repton preached utility, convenience, comfort and 'everything that conduces to the purpose of habitation with elegance', whereas Knight and Price campaigned for textures, character and picturesque effects (Plates 18, 19).

All three were agreed that reforms were necessary and Repton capably carried these out. Repton restored the Kitchen Garden to its rightful place and the terrace and a certain amount of formality near the house. His treatment of the Duke of Bedford's grounds at Woburn Abbey was typical. There he proposed a series of enclosed gardens near the house—an American Garden for American plants, a Chinese Garden decorated with the new oriental importations, a Botanic Garden, a Rosary, and forcing houses and greenhouses, as well as an English garden, or shrubbery walk, which connected the whole. The reason for the domestic differences between painting and garden which Repton mentioned are obvious. It was almost legal grounds for divorce. Dame Nature, Pope's classical goddess, now found herself confronted with exotic rivals from America, China and the tropics and something had to be done about it. Repton's solution was the seraglio where these beauties could be separated and sequestered, decently chaperoned by English shrubberies.

Repton's arguments on behalf of utility are understandable, too, if Brown's sacrifices of convenience for the sake of effect are taken into account. This had resulted in the sort of problem discussed by a writer of the period on the difficulties of guarding the windows of the house from cattle without obstructing the view with fences. It was suggested that the ground floor be raised, but Repton sensibly preferred the balustraded terrace and the keeping of cattle at a picturesque distance. Other familiar features which from this time made their appearance were the gravelled walk, in place of the common field path, rockeries, to provide a home for new Alpine importations, and the whole cult of rusticity—the rustic bridge, rustic seats, and rustic summer houses.

Repton as a landscape gardener is chiefly remembered for his ingenious water-colour slides, showing the estate before and after improvement—his 'Red Books' reports on his proposals, two hundred of which are recorded—and his publications, the chief of which were *Sketches and Hints on Landscape Gardening* (1795) and *An Inquiry into the Changes of Taste in Landscape Gardening* (1806). He was at one time in partnership with the architect John Nash. From contemporary prints and Repton's detailed Red Books it can be seen that this collaboration was a most successful one and resulted in some of the finest examples of English classic and Gothic architecture and landscape gardening. Repton's design for Regent's Park, laid out by Fordyce, the Surveyor-General in 1812, is a typical example of his style. He also designed the gardens in Cadogan and Russell Squares. His incursions into Hindoo architecture and decoration are reminiscent of Chambers' preoccupation with Chinese. Influenced by the publication of water-colours of Indian scenes by the Academicians, Thomas Daniell and William Hodges, he designed the house and garden of Sezincote. The result so attracted the Prince Regent that he commissioned him to prepare plans for a pavilion at Brighton. Though these were at first enthusiastically received, it was his old partner, Nash, who eventually supplanted him. Repton never got over the disappointment.

From the ideas of Repton and those of Price were evolved the nineteenth century park technique and the free planting of urban squares and crescents in the late Georgian and Regency periods. Perhaps these last were the most valuable contribution of all.

Within the next fifty years fundamental changes in values were to corrupt the free and innocent interplay of art and nature due to that fatal compromise, which Shenstone feared, when each invaded the other's province. The result was 'night, Gothicism, confusion and absolute chaos. . . .' For it was not long before architectural forms were to invade the garden and picturesque variety debase architecture and ornament.

47

THE STORY OF the English Landscape garden ends on a depressing note of confusion. And yet in spite of changes in fashion and taste, the imaginative compositions of Kent's school, the serpentine improvements of the 'Brunonian system', and the utilitarian and picturesque gardens of Repton's day, contributed to that rich and varied countryside of England of which the eighteenth century was so proud— that 'school of landscape' which inspired so many poets and painters in the silver age of English art. This achievement was well expressed by John Shebbeare in 1756 in his *Letters on the English Nation*. He wrote, 'The English have made a garden . . . a sensible consideration and adapted to all states which are incident to human minds in general. The gay and airy temper finds the open and cheerful spots of light . . . and the melancholy mood finds the solitary and shady grove, by the side of which slowly creeps the brook, complaining softly amongst the pebbles.'

In other words, the English had invented a new environment which was sensible, not only of visual values, but also of the reactions of such an environment on all states of the human mind in general. The irregular informal landscape tolerated and encouraged incongruity, the grotesque, surprise and variety, not from mere whimsy but because that was the way of nature and of liberty. It was the enemy of the monumental, of geometry, of regularity and the formal because that was artifice and autocracy.

PART II

DESCRIPTION OF GARDENS

CHISWICK PARK

THE GARDENS OF Chiswick Park are now a public park. They are, or they should be, a public monument. Here lies buried under bamboo, rhododendron and worn turf, the first of the experimental irregular gardens. The grounds are rich in association and historical memories. Pope and Gray, both young and both poets with reputations to make, were frequent visitors when the young Lord Burlington was building his bijou Palladian villa and laying out the grounds with the assistance of William Kent and Charles Bridgman, the royal gardener. From those days to this the gardens have undergone modifications and alterations to suit the prevailing taste, from Irregularity through both phases of the landscape park to the gardenesque period of the nineteenth century. But faint echoes still remain of those early days when Pope 'unloads the boughs within his reach' and of the two designers each directing the formation of their plantations, Bridgman's in a style later described as 'phlegmatic' and Kent's 'rural and cheerful'; of the laughter of the beautiful dancer Violetti, the adored wife of Garrick, and of the remonstrances of Lady Charlotte composing her fidgeting children to stillness in the garden before the canvas of Hogarth.

Lady Charlotte Boyle, daughter of Lord Burlington, is the link between the elegance of the Augustans and the carnival of the Georgian era, from the Burlington circle through nearly two hundred years of ownership by the Devonshires. It was her son who married, in 1774, the precocious Lady Georgiana, who in her 'teens had listened to Johnson and contested for the nearest place to his chair.

It was she who, after the birth of her first child, commissioned James Wyatt to enlarge the house and to transform the Palladian villa into an English home. Greatly talented she became a political muse who inspired and directed, politically and socially, the society of her day. The brilliant company that surrounded her to talk scandal, politics and laugh at the latest anecdote, listened to music, selected by Dr. Burney, in the grass amphitheatre under the shadow of Burlington's lovely temple (Frontispiece).

'Sweet Ches' became the centre of a web of Whig intrigue and politics during the crisis of the King's madness between November 1788 and the following January, when Grey, Townshend, Fox and Sheridan attempted to dethrone Pitt and seize power. It was to Chiswick and his friend the Duchess Georgiana that Charles James Fox came to die in 1806, while the devoted Sheridan whom he had declined to admit to his bedside paced the terrace beneath his room.

By the year 1816 the sixth Duke had bought the neighbouring property of Lady Coke and had built there a range of glass-houses and laid out a new formal flower garden in the neo-Italian style. About this period part of the property was leased to the new London Horticultural Society, later known as the Royal Horticultural Society. It remained their headquarters until they moved to their present premises.

Two of the illustrations reproduced here (Plates 29, 30) show the Cassina and the artificial river, which was probably Kent's first experiment in trying to reproduce the meanderings of a natural stream. The curves are only slight and both the stream and lake seem tentatively only to have overflowed from the canal and fish-pond motif of former days, not yet realizing perhaps the serpentine pleasures that were to come. Rocque's plan of 1736 is an excellent example of the Rococo irregular style (Plate 26). The main features of the garden were asymmetrically disposed on both sides of the main walks, each of which was terminated by a temple, the central

50

avenue leading to a semi-circular exedra of cut myrtle set in vases, and statues of Caesar, Pompey and Cicero, sad exiles from Hadrian's villa near Tivoli (Plate 28).

CASTLE HOWARD

IN THE OPINION of Geoffrey Webb, the editor of *The Complete Works of Sir John Vanbrugh* (1928), Castle Howard's gardens 'provide the link between the classic manner of Le Nôtre and certain traditions and influences from Holland . . . and the mid-eighteenth century aberrations of Pope, Kent and their landscape-gardening followers'. Though taking exception to the choice of his descriptive noun, it is a fair estimate of Vanbrugh's position in garden history. As this writer explains in a succeeding paragraph, Vanbrugh's great talent was in the composition of great vistas, and the placing of 'boscages' or organized woodlands. Certainly at Castle Howard Vanbrugh's genius for composition is still evident. The landscape is picturesque in its best and original sense.

Among the architectural decorations which led Walpole to exclaim that it was 'the grandest scene of real magnificence' were a castellated wall and intermediate towers along the skyline—a feature that delighted Vanbrugh's friends and about which Vanbrugh wrote to Lord Carlisle, with obvious amusement: 'They are all vastly surprised and taken with the wall and their towers, which they talk much of. I always thought we were sure of that card.'

Other features were an Ionic temple with four porticoes, a pyramid, another smaller temple, columns and obelisks. There was indeed a 'plantation' of small obelisks near the house, which was a great curiosity at the time, but which has, unfortunately, disappeared without trace. Greatest admiration was, however, reserved for the huge mausoleum which still dramatically dominates the landscape.

51

It was built by Hawkesmore and completed by Sir Thomas Robinson.

The romantic palace of towers, cupolas and domes (Plate 32) and the park with its classical and quasi-medieval garden buildings became a tourist Mecca throughout the century and descriptions appeared in contemporary diaries and books of travel such as those, for example, of Arthur Young.

WOBURN FARM

THE FIRST OF the great landscape gardens created by the 'proprietors of taste' was Woburn Farm (Plate 36). It consisted of about 150 acres of farmland in the Thames Valley near Chertsey, and was owned by Philip Southcote who purchased it in 1735. Thirty-five acres of this property, Southcote proceeded to improve, on original lines. The 'place contains 150 acres, of which near five and thirty are adorned to the highest degree; of the rest, about two-thirds are in pasture, and the remainder is in tillage; the decorations are, however, communicated to every part; for they are disposed along the sides of a walk, which, with its appendages, forms a broad belt round the grazing grounds, and is continued, though on a more contracted scale, through the arable. This walk is properly garden; all within is farm; the whole lies on two sides of a hill, and on a flat at the foot of it.'

It was the first example of the ornamented farm and was, I think, directly inspired by Joseph Addison's essay on Taste. Southcote did, in truth, make 'a pretty landscape of his own possessions', which was much admired by his contemporaries. Gray called it 'Southcote's Paradise, which, whenever you see it again, will improve upon you'. Whately's description is detailed, but is worth quoting fairly fully, particularly in view of the fact that The Leasowes, the most famous of the ornamented farms, to be described later, was a development of this first experiment.

52

'The flat is divided into cornfields; the pastures occupy the hill; they are surrounded by the walk, and crossed by a communication carried along the brow, which is also richly dressed, and which divides them into two lawns, each completely encompassed with garden.

'These are in themselves delightful; the ground in both lies beautifully; they are diversified with clumps and single trees, and the buildings in the walk seem to belong to them.'

The hills were crowned, of course, appropriately with temples, the ruin of a chapel, and a 'neat Gothic building' and the grounds were plentifully furnished with little seats and bridges. These decorations were to become familiar objects in the landscape garden.

'The buildings are not, however, the only ornaments of the walk; it is shut out from the country, for a considerable length of the way, by a thick and lofty hedgerow, which is enriched with woodbine, jessamine, and every odoriferous plant, whose tendrils will entwine with the thicket. A path, generally of sand or gravel, is conducted in a waving line, sometimes close under the hedge, sometimes at a little distance from it; and the turf on either hand is diversified with little groups of shrubs, or firs, or the smallest trees, and often with beds of flowers; these are rather too profusely strewed, and hurt the eye by their littleness; but then they replenish the air with their perfumes, and every gale is full of fragrancy.'

This winding walk passed round and enclosed the fields, changing its surface sometimes to grass, but always in every vacant space there was a rosary, 'a close or an open clump, or a bed of flowers'.

'If the parterre,' Whately continues, 'has been rifled for the embellishment of the fields, the country has, on the other hand, been searched for plants new in a garden; and the shrubs and the flowers which used to be deemed peculiar to the one, have been liberally transferred to the other.'

The mood invoked by the varied scenes was a happy one. 'A peculiar cheerfulness overspreads both the lawns, arising from the number and splendour of the objects with which they abound, the lightness of the buildings . . . and the varieties of the plantations. . . . The brow of the hill commands two lovely prospects; the one gay and extensive, over a fertile plain, watered by the Thames, and broken by St. Ann's Hill, and Windsor Castle . . . and every mark of opulence and cultivation. The other is more wooded; the steeple of a church, or the turrets of a seat, sometimes rises above the trees; and the bold arch of Walton Bridge is there a conspicuous object, equally singular and noble.'

The liveliness and rustic delights of farm life and of rural employment were watched and enjoyed by Philip Southcote's visitors strolling along the walks, while, resounding through the gardens, 'the lowing of the herds, the bleating of the sheep, and the tinklings of the bell-wether . . . even the clucking of poultry—for a menagerie of a very simple design was placed near the Gothic building—provided musical accompaniments to this pastoral scene'. Whately is, however, faintly disapproving, not on the grounds that perhaps agricultural efficiency may have been impaired, but because 'though so many of the circumstances occur, the simplicity of a farm is wanting . . . a rusticity of character cannot be preserved amidst all the elegant decorations which may be lavished on a garden'.

That Philip Southcote was a designer of originality and imagination, there is no doubt—though there is no other evidence of his work except a reference in a letter of Walpole's to 'Dr. Sayer's parsonage at Witham (Essex), which, with Southcote's help . . . he has made one of the most charming villas in England. There are sweet meadows falling down a hill, and rising on t'other side and the prettiest little winding stream you ever saw.'

Woburn Farm owed less to the pictorial, visual approach to landscape than most of the gardens to be described. It had its prospects, its Claudian temples and the like, but emphasis seems to have been laid more on providing a setting for a peaceful rural life. Connoisseurs of the day preferred the neighbouring estates of Esher Place or Claremont, where they found more variety both of mood and scene to the sunny cheerfulness of Woburn.

PAINS HILL

AT THE SAME TIME that Philip Southcote was ornamenting his farm, the Hon. Charles Hamilton at Pains Hill began his work of creating landscapes after the paintings of Poussin, and the Italian Masters. Nature was his inspiration. 'There may be scenes', said a contemporary, 'where nature has done more for herself, but in no place that I ever saw has so much been done for nature as at Pains Hill.'

Some of these gifts to nature were an artificial lake, considerably above the natural level of the valley, from which the water was drawn by a large cast-iron water-wheel; and an artificial grotto formed of spars and materials imported from Italy. The garden, and its temples, the grotto, and the lake, are still to be seen and the huge water-wheel still lifts the water from the 'silent Mole', the same stream that bounds Esher Place, as it did in the days of Hamilton. Recent photographs of Pains Hill and a description can be found in Mr. Tunnard's *Landscape and the Modern Garden*. Whately's description of the views from the Gothic building illustrated in this book are such as they are today, except that the trees, now full-grown, darken the lake (Plate 39): and obscure some of the vistas. 'An easy winding descent leads from the Gothic building to the lake, and a broad walk is afterwards continued along the banks and across an island, close to the water on one hand, and skirted by wood on the other; the spot is perfectly retired; but the retirement is cheerful;

55

the lake is calm: but it is full to the brim, and never darkened with shadow: the walk is smooth, and almost level, and touches the very margin of the water; the wood, which secludes all view into the country, is composed of the most elegant trees, full of the lightest greens, and bordered with shrubs and with flowers; and though the place is almost surrounded with plantations, yet within itself it is open and airy; it is embellished with three bridges, a ruined arch, and a grotto; and the Gothic building, still very near, and impending directly over the lake, belongs to the place; but these objects are never visible together; they appear in succession as the walk proceeds; and their number does not crowd the scene which is enriched by their frequency.'

Walpole divided gardens into three kinds, 'the garden that connects itself with a park . . . the ornamented farm, and . . . the forest or savage garden'. The three inventors of these types of gardens, he asserted, were Kent the first, Philip Southcote the second, and Mr. Charles Hamilton at Pains Hill for the third type, 'that kind of Alpine scenery, composed almost solely of pines and firs, a few birch, and such trees as assimilate with a savage and mountainous country'.

This slice of the Alps, closely modelled on the drawings of Salvator Rosa, was made at the head of the lake, but has today lost all its savage charm, the reason being that pines and firs are now indigenous to the Surrey landscape and have lost their associations with wild and mountainous country—but Hamilton's virtuosity at handling such scenes was admired by his contemporaries. He worked, perhaps more deliberately and directly than others, from Pope's dictum that 'all gardening is Landscape painting'. He made for his friend the Marquis of Lansdowne at Bowood a cascade from a picture by Gasper Poussin (Plate 55), and assisted James Fox with the grounds of his villa at St Ann's Hill. The pictorial effects he achieved in these grounds and at Pains Hill were extraordinarily

56

skilful, as can be seen today now that his planting has reached full maturity; but they were for the most part only painters' landscapes and, at Pains Hill, do not consciously seem to have been made to invoke any of those moods, so dear to the eighteenth century man of taste, of gaiety, melancholy, or enchantment. Sublimity was achieved in the 'savage garden' and perhaps in the dark recess of the huge grotto—but for variety, Hamilton's contemporaries travelled to the gardens set among the wild and romantic scenery and the wide prospects of Worcestershire, Staffordshire and Shropshire.

THE LEASOWES

FEW MEN WERE so much beloved and respected by their contemporaries as William Shenstone, poet and landscape gardener. The Leasowes was, it was said, 'a perfect picture of his mind, simple, elegant and amiable'. His estate was a small farm, which he inherited, with three hundred pounds a year, from his mother's family. Its care and cultivation occupied most of his life and from the time when he left Oxford to his death he seldom left it. The Leasowes became to Shenstone's contemporaries the Sabine Farm of their Horatian ideal, and his solitary life in pastoral surroundings was the subject of as much curiosity as Beckford's monastic silence at Fonthill to a later generation. The Leasowes attracted to its walks and groves, statesmen, poets, and many of the most interesting and famous characters of the eighteenth century. A list of visitors would include Burke and Adam Smith, William Pitt, Horace Walpole, the Lytteltons from Hagley, Thomas Percy (Editor of *The Reliques of Ancient English Poetry*), Rev. Joseph Spence, James Thomson, Wesley, Goldsmith and Samuel Johnson. And such a list reveals the attraction which nature and natural beauty had for the eighteenth

57

century character and how wide was this passion for creating land-scapes. For these visitors were not only sight-seers, for most of them were already engaged in improving their own properties and had

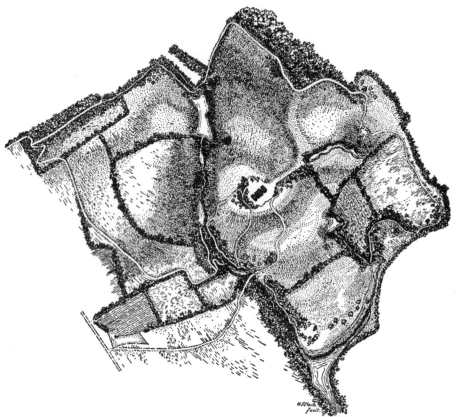

Plan of The Leasowes by the author after R. Dodsley, 1765

come to the Leasowes for inspiration. William Pitt's garden at Enfield Chase was well known and his advice had been taken by Lyttelton during the making of Hagley; Joseph Spence was an enthusiastic gardener as well as the author of the *Anecdotes*, Oliver

Goldsmith contributed to the *Public Ledger* essays which revealed more than a superficial knowledge of English and Chinese landscape gardening, while James Thomson, poet of the landscape and all her seasons, praised The Leasowes extravagantly, proposed alterations and invited Shenstone to his house at Richmond. Boswell and Samuel Johnson's visit was made after Shenstone's death, in 1774. In an entry in the journal of their journey into North Wales for September of that year, it is noted that it was raining at the time but that they visited all the waterfalls. 'There are, in one place, fourteen falls in a short line.' This was possibly all the more noticeable as a feature of the place, since they had just previously visited Hagley, where it was observed that the place 'wants water'. But Johnson, no lover of country life and not at all susceptible to the new fashion for rural improvement (according to Mrs. Thrale, 'he hated to hear about prospects and views, and laying out ground and taste in gardening'), justly remarked about Shenstone's activities that whether such work 'demands any great powers of mind, I will not inquire . . . perhaps a sullen and surly spectator may think such performances rather the sport than the business of human reason. But it must be at least confessed, that to embellish the form of nature is an innocent amusement; and some praise must be allowed, by the most supercilious observer, to him who does best what such multitudes are contending to do well.' Johnson confirmed what was the general opinion, that Shenstone, on his small estate and with the scantiest means, had created landscapes unmatched by any of his contemporaries.

Though Johnson would not admit that landscape gardening was anything more than innocent amusement, he implied in his short essay on Shenstone, included in the *Lives of English Poets*, that The Leasowes was perhaps as much the lyrical expression of Shenstone, the poet, as any of his verses—for The Leasowes was an Arcadia, an elegant eighteenth century edition of that ideal, which provided a vehicle for his moods, and a stimulus to creative activity—just as these landscapes were in turn the conscious expression of his poetic fancy.

His name for the form he developed was a *ferme ornée*. The name was adopted, so he said, from the French *parc orné*. The Leasowes was a direct result of Southcote's ornamented farm at Woburn. Ideas borrowed from Woburn Farm by a Mr. Morgan of Essex were in turn copied by a relative, Morgan Graves of Mickleton. The results are said by Richard Graves to have been rather indifferent, but they were 'sufficient to engage the attention and excite the active imagination of Mr. Shenstone'. Hagley, in his neighbourhood, was at this time being improved, but on so large a scale that Shenstone would not have been tempted to copy any of its features. Richard Graves in his *Recollection of some Particulars in the Life of the Late William Shenstone, Esq.*, published in 1788, a source for some contemporary books on Shenstone, wrote that, before visiting the Graves at Mickleton, Shenstone had 'cut a straight walk through his wood, terminated by a small building of rough stone; and in a sort of gravel or marle pit, in the corner of a field, amongst some hazels, he had scooped out a sort of cave, stuck a little cross of wood over the door, and called it an hermitage; and, a few years after, had built an elegant little summer-house in the water, under the fine group of beeches (which was afterwards removed by Mr. Pitt's advice)'.

It was only after his visit to Mickleton and after these regrettable experiments that he began to work to a consistent plan and to ring his property with what was described as 'a walk as unadorned as a common field path'. It appeared to be only a very humble relation of Southcote's ornamented and ornamental belt, but, in the opinion of Whately, it was better suited to the simplicity of a farm.

Shenstone's common field path linked a variety of natural scenes —cascades, a lake, lawns, dells, groves of trees, hills and rural valleys—a lovers' walk—and wide prospects over the surrounding landscape. Shenstone's lack of means prevented him from decorating his grounds with the temples and buildings which his contemporaries so lavishly scattered over their estates. The Leasowes contained, however, a Temple of Pan, frankly called by an admirer 'indisputably a blot to The Leasowes', and the Priory ruin, which, the disapproving Whately said, 'has no peculiar beauty to recommend it'. Shenstone toyed with the fashionable taste for 'Gothic' but not with the whole-hearted enthusiasm, or obviously the success, of some of his friends. Though unadorned by buildings, the walk was plentifully supplied with seats, inscriptions and urns. These urns were, said Whately, 'the favourite embellishment of The Leasowes; they are indeed among the principal ornaments of the place; for the buildings are mostly mere seats, or little root-houses'. However, the writer considered a multiplicity of objects unnecessary in a farm where the surrounding prospects were full of them—such as, presumably, church steeples, clustering villages and Hagley's sham castle, on the skyline.

These seats were extremely important objects in the landscape and like those at Hagley they were supplied with lines of verse. In a poem written by Dodsley, after his first visit, he calls them 'incantations':

> . . . 'And see, the spells,
> The powerful incantations, magic verse,
> Inscribed on every tree, alcove, or urn.'

These were, of course, spells and incantations to charm the visitor into a receptive mood or to provide a clue to the emotion which the scene was intended to invoke.

'Divine oblivion of low-thoughted care' was inscribed, for instance, on a bench at the foot of a precipice, adapted, said Heely, 'to contemplate the savage, gloomy wilderness, that everywhere surrounds it'.

One called 'The Assignation Seat' carried some suitable lines by Wharton:

> 'O Galatea! Nymph that swans more bright,
> More sweet than thyme, more fair than ivory white:
> When pastured herds at evening seek the stall,
> Haste to my arms! nor scorn thy lover's call.'

Joseph Heely, who wrote a detailed description in his *Letters on the Beauties of Hagley, Envil and The Leasowes* in 1777, confessed that 'he could not sit without indulging a thousand agreeable ideas —everything around me seemed calculated to infuse the tenderest, warmest wishes—concealment—delicious shade-spreading trees—a calm transparent stream—to the ear, the soft melody of the adjoining grove, and the distant tinkling of a fairy rill'.

That these seats were considered something more than merely resting places is argued by Heely. A bench rather close to another in Virgil's Grove was objected to by critics for the reason that since it was so near, it must therefore be redundant. 'A resting place!' said the indignant Heely. 'A resting place! How careful should everyone be in making himself perfectly acquainted with a work before he presumes, in any respect, to criticize! How would Mr. Shenstone have laughed at, pitied, and despised such miserable commentators. One would imagine it palpable to every eye for what purpose this spot was chosen to draw the spectator to—surely to show the diversity, taste, and what the natural Genius of the place had to give, within the distance of a few paces!'

Virgil's Grove was the principal attraction of The Leasowes. 'None ever beheld this grove, without a thorough sense of satisfaction; and were one to chuse any one particular spot of this perfectly Arcadian Farm, it would be this,' said Robert Dodsley. Whately called it 'enchanting', and Heely: 'It is all beauty, and that productive of everything to give the imagination and fasten the eye in delight.'

62

It is worth quoting parts of Heely's description of this place of pilgrimage. At the entrance was a small obelisk, under the shade of some oaks dedicated 'to the genius of Virgil' and a seat on the back of which was an inscription to James Thomson. 'The whole of the grove here opens in all its glory—your eye, greedy to catch every object at a glance, knows not where to rest; for to fix its predominant beauty is impossible. . . . The boldest object . . . is a noble cascade, plunging down a rude shelve of rock, within a sort of grot, darkened and overshaded by thicket and shrubs; the fall is bold, luxuriant, and sonorous, naturally forming a frothy basin below; on the brink of which, a Venus, supposed either going to lave, or just emerged, stands in modest attitude, seemingly listening, and conscious of her exposed charms. . . . Immediately opposite, appears a grotesque fountain, dripping its shower from the crevices of a rough rocky niche, grown over with scummy aquatic weeds—behind this, and indeed the whole dell . . . is closely feathered with thicket; while within, its almost perpendicular banks and bottom are filled with stately spreading trees . . . these, inter-weaving their branches within the arms of the larger forest oaks and beeches, throw a solemn gloomy cast around, impervious to the sun except by some casual openings, where his rays dart through, and beautifully chequer the surface of the ground with its enlivening contrast.'

'Filled with the deepest attention' Heely moved to a near-by bench, that seat which was the subject of so much controversy. The view from this place 'catches the rambling mazes of the rivulet in a different character, stealing more quietly along in careless simplicity; no arch, no obelisk, no dripping fountain—all are artfully excluded'.

Leaving this seat, and walking further in the grove, the scene became darkened by yew trees. The path leads to a 'root-house in a melancholy obscurity; where you will please yourself with reading the following well-adapted lines'. These informed the visitor that this was the dwelling-place of 'fays and faeries' and warned him to behave himself in language slightly more elegant than that usually seen in our own public parks:

> ' . . . tread with awe these favour'd bowers,
> Nor wound the shrubs, nor bruise the flowers;
> So may your path with sweets abound;
> So may your couch with rest be crowned;
> But harm betide the wayward swain,
> Who dares our hallow'd haunts profane.'

Heely confessed that it would be 'perhaps as well, if both the cell and walk were unknown' and called it a 'dead and gloomy track'—an opinion which appeared to be justified. Returning on the other side of this glen various new views were seen of the stream and cascade—a closer inspection was made of the 'grot'—'which to give, in stronger colours its character as a grotto, a rude seat, composed of stone, under rugged roots is introduced with strict propriety'. This seat was inscribed:

> 'The haunt of Nereids, fram'd by nature's hands;
> Where polish'd seats appear of living stone,
> And limpid rills, that tinkle as they run.'

The Venus appears once more, and verses addressed to her are found, engraved on the brink of a basin. These lines contain advice on landscape gardening,[1] abjuring all 'boastful sons of taste' to learn modesty and reserve from this bashful 'beauty'. The most interesting line is the reference to 'China's vain alcoves'. By this time Chinoiserie was 'in full blow' in fashionable London, and Chinese temples were appearing with classical and Gothic in English gardens —much to Shenstone's disapproval.

---

[1]Shenstone was the inventor of the expression Landscape Gardener. He wrote in *Unconnected Thoughts* . . . 'Gardeners may be divided into three sorts, the landskip gardener, the parterre gardener and the kitchen gardener . . . I have used the word landskip gardener, because, in pursuance of our present taste in gardening, every good painter of landskip appears to me the most proper designer.' Shenstone, *The Works* . . . 2 Vols. 2nd Ed. 1765. Vol II. pp. 123-4.

Learn hence, ye boastful sons of taste,
    Who plan the rural shade;
Learn hence, to shun the vicious waste
    Of pomp, at large displayed.

Let sweet concealment's magic art
    Your mazy bounds invest;
And while the sight unveils a part,
    Let fancy paint the rest.

Let coy reserve with cost unite,
    To grace your wood or field;
No ray obtrusive pall the sight,
    In ought you plant, or build.

And far be driven the sumptuous glare
    Of gold, from British groves;
And far the meritricious air
    Of China's vain alcoves.

'Tis bashful beauty ever twines
    The most coercive chain;
'Tis she, that sovereign rule declines
    Who best deserve to reign.

Modesty and reserve, sweet concealment, and elegance, were adjectives generally applied to Shenstone's rural shades and 'the sumptuous glare of gold' appeared no nearer to The Leasowes presumably than the gates of Hagley. The general opinion of visitors was that The Leasowes was the perfect model of gardening —as well as a new form. For though Woburn Farm was its parent there was little similarity between a common field path and an ornamental belt, and no other garden matched its simplicity.

CLAREMONT

CLAREMONT IS ONE of those eighteenth century landscape gardens which were praised by contemporary men of taste as an 'Elysium' or a 'Parnassus'. Both Walpole and Whately were enthusiastic. It is chiefly interesting as one of the few gardens which were improved, successively, by three of the best known men connected with the landscape movement, namely, Sir John Vanbrugh, William Kent, and 'Capability' Brown. Briefly, the history of the estate is as follows:

Vanbrugh bought the estate and built himself a house there in about 1700. He afterwards sold it to Thomas Pelham, the Earl of Clare and the future Duke of Newcastle. After buying up and enclosing some of the surrounding property, he commissioned Kent to lay out the grounds. A plan of 1717 shows a castellated garden house on the mount and the addition of the lake under its shadow was a feature added during his occupation. Kent's gardens aroused the usual enthusiasm, moving, for example, the poet-physician, Dr. Samuel Garth, to write another of his mock heroic poems on its beauties.

After the death of the Duke, Claremont was bought by the wealthy nabob, Lord Clive, who, before returning for his last visit to India, directed Brown to pull down the old mansion, build a new house, and remodel the grounds.

Geo. Barrett's view is of the result (Plate 42). Lord Clive's admonishment that the house was to command 'fine prospects from the four fronts' may have prompted Brown to eliminate the usual service entrance by sinking the kitchen and servants' quarters in a deep basement and to build a subterranean approach to the servants' entry under the encircling lawn.

As viewed today, what remains of the result of the work of Vanbrugh, Kent and Brown is certainly charming. The wooded mount and the lake (Plate 43), now ringed with rhododendron, are made the more romantic by the half-covered ruins of a garden temple on the lake island and evidences of other garden buildings on the slopes of the mount. The open glades are, unhappily, pegged out for future 'development'. Vanbrugh's stables and the old walled kitchen garden are already, as is the rest of the estate, 'developed'.

STOWE

K ENT MAY HAVE BEEN 'Kentissime' at Esher, but at Stowe he assisted Bridgman and Lord Cobham to create a scene of 'more than mortal magnificence', 'an Albano landscape' of 'inexpressible richness'. Enough to make every poetaster during the century exclaim in doggerel and verse in lines such as these:

'Oh, how charming the walks to my fancy appear,
What a number of temples and grottos are here!'

or in the heroic, classical vein:

'Such, as when Poussin's or Albano's hand,
On glowing canvas the rich landscape plann'd,
And classic genius strove by mimic art,
Thro' the admiring eye to reach the heart.

'Here the fair queen of this heroic isle,
Imperial Albion, with a gracious smile,
Confess'd, she lovely nature saw, at last,
Unite with art, and both improve by taste.'

In an area of four hundred acres and assisted by such talent as Vanbrugh, James Gibbs, Bridgman and Kent, Lord Cobham created a garden which achieved as great a European reputation as Le Nôtre's gardens at Versailles, and set the fashion in the courts of Europe for the *Jardin Anglais.*

In the series of plans reproduced, the slow development of the landscape at Stowe is clearly shown. The gardens were first begun in 1713 (Plate 45). The layout was formal near the house, which was flanked by flower gardens. A wide central vista led to the lake from which cross vistas merged into the wilderness of the home park. Bridgman's designs are shown in a plan and a series of engravings by Rigaud and Baron, and published in 1739. He was also responsible probably for the great boundary walk of gravel of about three or four miles in circumference which he planted with rows of trees and with a sunk fence between it and the outer park—an idea which some years later a young under-gardener at Stowe, called Brown, possibly noted for future use[1].

Kent's influence is clearly seen in the second plan (Plate 46). Much of the parterre, and the formal gardens near the house were swept away. Broad vistas were opened out to reveal the temples now

[1]Lancelot Brown was employed for thirteen years as garden boy and, later, as head gardener. He left in 1750. There is no evidence that he had any hand in the designing of Stowe. Lord Cobham restricted him to the kitchen and flower garden.

framed by well-established trees. The river (and lake) was made to serpentine 'seemingly at its pleasure, and where discontinued by different levels, its course appeared to be concealed by thickets properly interspersed, and glittered again at a distance where it might be supposed naturally to arrive. Its sides were smoothed, but preserved their meanderings.' In the third plan (Plate 48) there is a little trace of formality left, only 'prospect, animated prospect' dominates the scene.

The pride of Stowe was its rich display of temples and buildings. No less than thirty-eight[1] of these dotted the landscape. 'If Stowe had but half so many buildings as it has, there would be too many,' wrote Walpole, but confessed that 'that profusion, that glut enriches, and makes it look like a fine landscape of Albano; one figures one-self in Tempe or Daphne'.

It was these temples and buildings which drew to the place sight-seers from most of the courts of Europe. During the visit of Princess Amelia, Walpole wrote an account of the entertainments provided: 'A small Vauxhall was acted for us at the Grotto in the Elysian Fields,[2] which was illuminated with lamps, as were the thicket and

---

[1]The temples and buildings at Stowe from various contemporary sources: Corinthian Arch (Thomas Pitt, Lord Camelford). The Queen's Building (Kent). The Hermitage (Kent). Temple of Venus (Kent). Gateway (Kent). Temple of Ancient Virtue (Kent). The Shell Bridge (Kent). Temple of British Worthies (Kent). Congreve's Monument (Kent). Temple of Concord and Victory (Kent)—later altered by Barra. Two Entrance Pavilions (Kent, Barra). The Rotunda (Vanbrugh). Boycott Pavilions (Vanbrugh). Temple of Bacchus (Vanbrugh). The Gothic Temple (Gibbs). Lord Cobham's Pillar (Gibbs). Captain Grenville's Monument. A Tower. The Castle. An Obelisk to the Memory of General Wolfe. The Grotto. The Cold Bath. Gateway (Leoni). Queen Caroline Monument. King Geo. II Monument. Dido's Cave. Nelson's Seat. Coucher's Obelisk. St. Augustine's Cave. The Fane of Diane. Egyptian Pyramid in Memory of Vanbrugh. Artificial Rockwork. Palladian Bridge. Temple of Friendship. Equestrian Statue of George I. Pebble Alcove. The Witch House. Temple of Modern Virtue (a Ruin). The Bourbon Tower (1808). Doric Arch (1766) inscribed to Princess Amelia.
(Architects where known given in brackets.)

[2]A valley where the figures of 'heroes, poets and philosophers, seem to justify the name. This part is watered by a small rivulet, which, flowing from the grotto, passes through a valley orna-mented with a number of fine old trees, and then empties itself into the lake. The valley includes some of the most charming views and objects in the whole district.'

two little banks on the lake,' and of the chief entertainment, which was a visit to an arch which Lord Cobham had erected in her honour: 'It is placed on an eminence at the top of the Elysian Fields, in a grove of orange-trees. You come to it on a sudden, and are startled with delight on looking through it; you at once see, through a glade, the river winding at the bottom; from which a thicket rises, arched over with trees, but opened, and discovering a hillock full of haycocks, beyond which in front is the Palladian Bridge and again over that a larger hill crowned with a castle. It is a tall landscape framed by the arch and the over-bowering trees, and comprehending more beauties of light, shade, and buildings than any picture of Albano I ever saw.'

Such were the pictures painted by Kent and his assistants, but that is not all we would expect to find. Remembering Addison's dictum that a garden provides 'innumerable subjects for meditation' it is not surprising to read that Walpole was stimulated to moralize:

'The number of buildings and variety of scenes in the garden made each day different from the rest: and my meditations on so historic a spot prevented my being tired. Every acre brings to one's mind some instance of the parts or pedantry, of the taste or want of taste, of the ambition or love of fame, or greatness or miscarriages, of those who have inhabited, decorated, planned or visited the place. Pope, Congreve, Vanbrugh, Kent, Gibbs, Lord Cobham, Lord Chesterfield, the mob of nephews, the Lyttletons, Grenvilles, Wests, Leonidas Glover and Wilkes, the late Prince of Wales, the King of Denmark, Princess Amelia, and the proud monuments of Lord Chatham's services, now enshrined there, then anathematized there, and now again commanding there, with the Temple of Friendship, like the Temple of Janus, sometimes open to war, and sometimes shut up in factious cabals—all these images crowd upon one's memory, and add visionary personages to the charming scenes, that are so enriched with fanes and temples, that the real prospects are little less than visions themselves.'

70

This then is the essence of the new art, 'the real prospects' appear as 'little less than visions'. It is an art that requires, therefore, the interaction of artist and observer. An observer, educated and cultured enough to understand the associations and interpret the allusions offered to him. That this was the recognized approach is clear from a description of Stowe written in the form of a dialogue by an anonymous visitor in 1751: '... Men of all taste, he said, might here meet with something to their taste. The thoughtful might find retired Walks for contemplation. The Gay and Airy might see Nature in her loveliest dress, and meet objects corresponding with their liveliest Flights. The Romantic Genius might entertain itself with objects in its own way, and grow wild with ideas of the enchanted kind. The Man of true Taste might enjoy a noble Entertainment; and even the trifling Genius (such condescension was there here to all Persons) might pick out something for his Amusement. In a word, says he, these gardens are a good Epitome of the World: They give free Scope to Inclinations of every Kind; and if in some Parts they humour the Sensualists' debauched Taste, in others they pay very noble compliments to Virtue—but what chiefly pleased him, was the amicable Conjunction of Art and Nature through the whole: The former, he observed, was never stiff, nor the latter extravagant. Here Callophilus, interposing, said, in this Point he must differ from him: If Censure was due to anything here, in his opinion, it was to a too great Profusion of Ornament: The Simplicity of Nature, he thought, indeed was too much polished away.'

That was the general opinion of many of his contemporaries who preferred more subtle and rural charms to such elaborate magnificence. But Stowe is important to garden historians for its influence on the Continent and because its success established the new movement and stimulated other owners of large estates to carry out similar improvements.

NUNEHAM PARK

NUNEHAM PARK was the property of Viscount Nuneham, Lord Harcourt. Horace Walpole became very friendly with the family and was a frequent visitor to the house. He seemed particularly pleased to have found in Lady Harcourt a versifier of merit and so modest that she would never allow her friends to read her poems. Lord Harcourt appeared to be equally talented as an etcher, his work appearing to Walpole to be 'superior in boldness and freedom of stroke to anything we have seen from established artists'. It is not surprising, therefore, to find that the Harcourts, poet and artist, were also gardeners and that their park had been improved by Lancelot Brown. What distinguished it from other estates laid out by Brown, was the fact that it possessed also a large flower garden, which had the merit of delighting Walpole, who might have been as equally shocked as he was at most departures from the prevailing mode. Other landscape parks had had flower gardens, but these were laid out in the traditional 'compartments' and hidden away with the kitchen garden like 'the wilderness of sweets' at Blenheim, which was a copy of La Pompadour's garden at Versailles. The Nuneham flower garden was laid out by the poet William Mason, author of *The English Garden*, and was informal. From contemporary engravings, two of which are reproduced (Plates 51, 52), the planting of the flower borders seems to have been well in advance of current practice. Most of the available perennials were grouped in much the same way as is the fashion today. Walpole called it delightedly 'the quintessence of nosegays'. 'I wonder', he wrote to Mason, 'that some Maccaroni does not offer ten thousand pounds for it', and, in another letter to the Countess of Upper Ossory, he remarked that it was 'a flower garden that would keep all Maccaronia in nosegays'.

The gardener was one William Clark, who pleased Walpole so

72

Page facing
The Deserted Village by Bewick from W. Bulmer,
poems by Goldsmith Parnell, 1795

much that he wrote asking the Harcourts if 'your Linnaeus should have any disciple that would condescend to look after my little Flower Garden, it would be the delight of my eyes and nose'.

This garden of an acre and a quarter contained, as well as nose-gays, busts of Frances Poole, Cowley, Prior, Locke, and of Rousseau, each with an appropriate inscription, and also inscriptions on seats and tablets from the works of Dryden, Marvel, Milton, Whitehead and Mason. The first two lines of the dedication to Mason on a cinerary urn might indeed summarize the essence of the whole art of landscape gardening in the eighteenth century.

> 'The poet's feeling and the painter's eye,
> In this thy lov'd retreat, we pleas'd descry.'

It would also be appropriate to mention that there occurred at Nuneham one of those ruthless seizures under the Enclosure Acts of the eighteenth century by which the Harcourts appropriated the whole village of Nuneham in order to bring the land under Brown's scheme of improvement. The village church was destroyed and the cottages razed to the ground. The church was rebuilt in 1764 by the architect Stuart, 'as a noble ornament to the pleasure ground', in the form of a Roman Temple 'which besides its utility as a place of worship is rendered a very desirable object'. The Harcourts accommodated the villagers on another site on the London Road, building, so it was said, a sufficient number of houses for them.

WOBURN ABBEY

IN THE *Enquiry into Changes of Taste in Landscape Gardening* by Humphrey Repton, Woburn Abbey is given as an example of a modern garden in 1806. The innovations introduced by Repton reflect the changes which had by then taken place in the eighteenth century landscape composition. In place of the 'vapid smoothness' of Brown, the encircling lawn near the mansion, the terrace and parterre returned to its old position, and another exile, the traditional Italian *giardino segreto* or the secret garden, was introduced for the private use of the owner. As has been said in previous pages, Repton's solution to the difficult problem of assimilating the new plants which by then were flooding the country was to segregate them into separated units. At Woburn these were, the Rosary, or 'dressed flower garden', the American Garden, for North American shrubs, the Chinese Garden, for Chinese introductions, the Botanic Garden for scientific classification, the Animated Garden or Menagerie (Plate 54), and the English Garden or shrubbery walk connecting the whole.

These small enclosed gardens, which in the English gardens of the seventeenth century were usually disposed formally on each side of a central axis, were, in the nineteenth century, 'secluded from the natural scenery . . .' a kind of episode to the great and more conspicuous parts of the place, for Repton, true child of the period, held that landscape gardening should 'studiously conceal every appearance of art, however expensive. . . .'

Amongst the attractions of Woburn Abbey was a Chinese Dairy, built by Henry Holland in 1789. The windows were painted with Chinese figures and the lake, by which it stood, was planted with the Chinese novelties of the day, rhododendrons, azaleas, China roses and hydrangeas. Close to this was a Children's Garden designed by Repton, which was ingeniously subdivided into individual gardens, each with a separate arbour on which was the name of the owner. It also contained a grotto, inlaid with shells in the traditional manner.

The park, which contained about one hundred acres of evergreens planted in 1742, was rendered picturesque by Repton with winding lakes, spacious walks and rides and lodges. One of these lodges, Aspley Cottage, was built by Repton's son.

In 1833, James Forbes, the Duke of Bedford's gardener, wrote an interesting descriptive catalogue of the plants at Woburn Abbey, listing over six thousand ornamental plants as well as describing the various new glass-houses, which must have been an innovation in those days. There were greenhouses and a conservatory for natives of the Cape, Japan and the East Indies, a Heathery, built from the designs of Jeffry Wyatville for the new Cape Heaths, a Peach House, Vinery, Pinery and forcing pits for melons and cucumbers as well as a mushroom house. In these new stove houses were the colourful and strangely marked coleus and crotons and other exotic foliage plants which fairly soon after this were to invade the parterres and green lawns of English country houses and city parks and form the basis for the elaborate carpet bedding schemes of the Victorians.

TEXT ILLUSTRATIONS

The achievement of the eighteenth century landscape gardeners can be well illustrated by comparisons of formal gardens as engraved by Johannes Kip in 1708 and those of his successor in Gloucestershire, Thomas Bonnor. The Kip engravings were first published in 1708 in *Britannia Illustrata*. The Bonnor, Chesham, and Benazeck engravings were published between 1771 and 1780 for inclusion in Samuel Rudder's *A New History of Gloucestershire*, a good example of the landscape influence on the majority of large country houses.

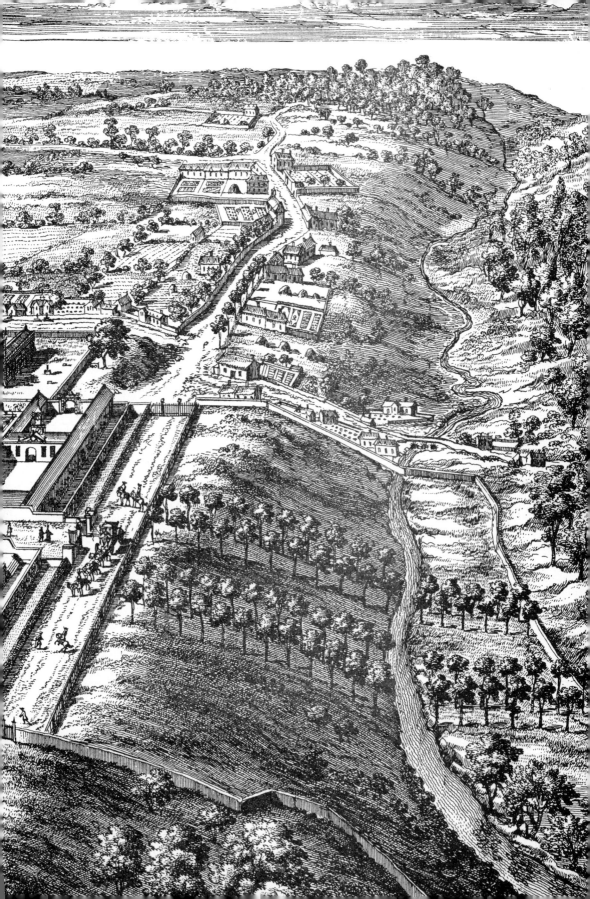

THE PLATES

1 Claude Lorraine: Sketch for Landscape

2 Claude Lorraine: Sketch for Landscape. The source of the forms used in the Landscape Park; arching trees, lake water, picturesque ruins

3   Claude Lorraine: Study of trees

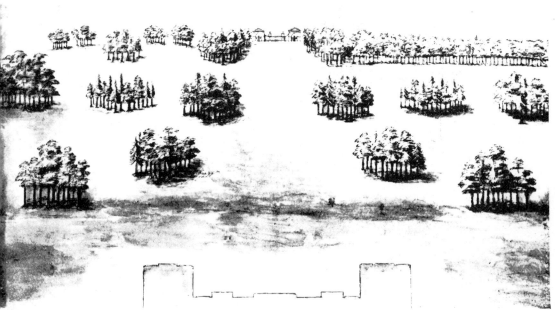

4   Holkham Hall, Norfolk: Sketch by William Kent. The invention of clump planting. *Lord Leicester Collection, Holkham*

5   Hare Hall, Essex: Engraving by W. Angus after Thomas Day, 1791

6   Hagley Park, Worcestershire: Engraving by T. Mathews after J.P. Neale

7 Dalkeith Palace, Scotland: Engraving by W. Angus after Geo. Barrett, 1788

Ruine de Kew vue par le Nord.

8 Artificial Ruin at Kew Gardens by William Chambers from *Détails de Nouveaux Jardins à la mode*, by Le Rouge, Paris, 1776-87

9   Ranston, Dorsetshire: Engraved by W. Watts after T. Hearne, 1779

10   Halswell, Somerset: Engraved by W. Watts after J. Richards R.A., 1780

11 Kew Gardens: A view of the Wilderness and the Alhambra, the Pagoda and the Mosque. Engraved by E. Rooker after William Marlowe

12 Kew Gardens: A view of the Palace at Kew from the Lawn. Engraving by William Woollett after J. Kirby

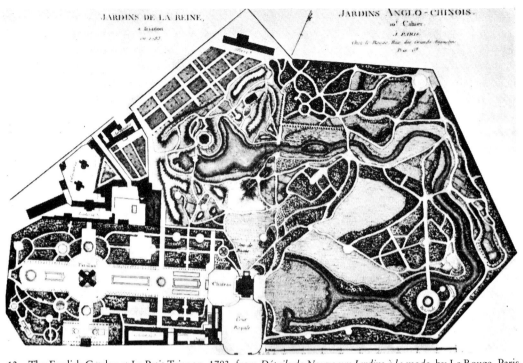

13 The English Garden at Le Petit Trianon, 1783, from *Détails de Nouveaux Jardins à la mode*, by Le Rouge, Paris, 1776-87

14 Blenheim Palace: Engraving by W. Angus after Lord Duncannon, 1787

15   A Gentleman's Park: An unidentified wash drawing by Humphry Repton

16 Sheffield Place, Sussex: Engraving by W. Watts after P. Sandby, R.A., 1779

17 Sheffield Place, Sussex: Engraving by W. Angus after Humphry Repton, 1791

18 Engraving from drawing by Richard Payne Knight, from *The Landscape, A Didactic Poem in Three Books*, by R.P. Knight, 1794, Plate I

19 As above, the garden 'dressed in the modern style'. Brown's 'shaven lawns'

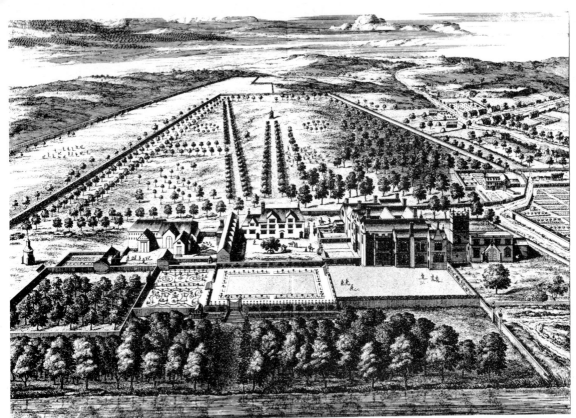

20   Barrington, Gloucestershire: Drawn and engraved by J. Kip, 1708

21   Barrington, Gloucestershire: The Landscape Park, showing garden temple and a bridge in the Chinese manner. Drawn and engraved by Thomas Bonnor, 1772

22 Chiswick House: Design for the Cascade by William Kent. Pen and wash drawing. *Duke of Devonshire Collection, Chatsworth*

DIVERSES GROTTES.
Chinoises et autres

23 Designs for Grottoes in various styles from *Détails de Nouveaux Jardins à la mode*, by Le Rouge, Paris, 1776-87

24　Rousham, Oxfordshire: *Country Life*

25　As above. A Garden Glade and a Garden Building by William Kent. *Country Life*

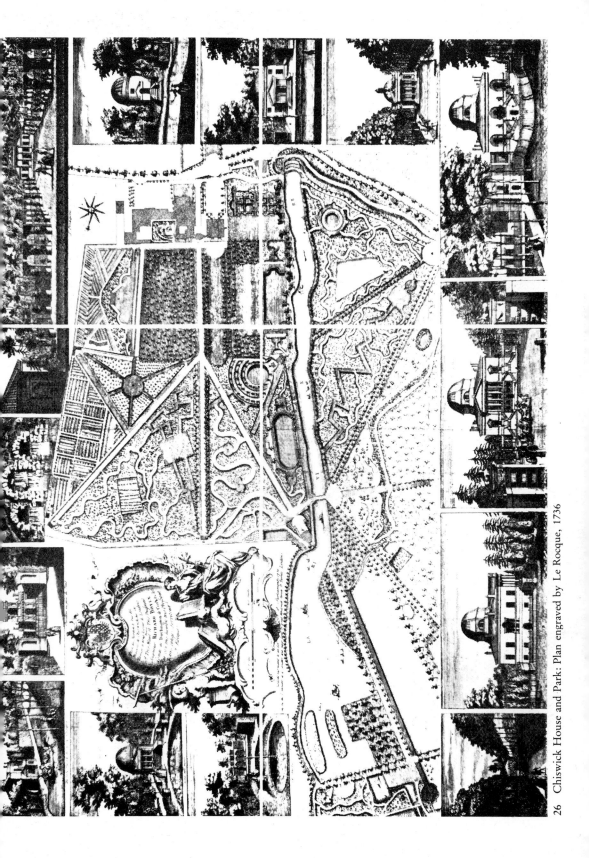

26 Chiswick House and Park: Plan engraved by Le Rocque, 1736

27　Chiswick House: Design for Exedra by William Kent. Pen and wash drawing. *Copyright of the Duke of Devonshire*

28　Chiswick House: The Exedra as it is today. *P.W. Hammond*

29 Chiswick House: View of the House and Garden showing William Kent's Cascade. Engraving from *The Modern Universal British Traveller*, 1779. *Courtesy London Borough of Hounslow, Chiswick Library*

30 Chiswick House: View of the Cassina and Serpentine River. Engraving from *The Modern Universal British Traveller*, 1779. *Courtesy of London Borough of Hounslow, Chiswick Library*

31   The Column at Chiswick. *P.W. Hammond*

Castle Howard, Yorkshire: Engraving by W. Angus after William Marlowe, 1787

Castle Howard, Yorkshire: A Vanbrugh Landscape. *Country Life*

34 Castle Howard, Yorkshire: The Ionic Temple by Sir John Vanbrugh. *Country Life*

35 Castle Howard, Yorkshire: The Mausoleum by Hawkesmore and Sir Thomas Robinson. *Country Life*

6 Wooburn Farm, Surrey: Contemporary engraving after S. Wale. *Surrey County Library*

37 Wooburn Farm, Surrey: The Ornamental Farm, engraving after Luke Sullivan. *Surrey County Library*

38　Pains Hill, Surrey: The Gothic Tent

39　Pains Hill, Surrey, The Artificial Ruin and Lake

40 Pains Hill, Surrey: Charles Hamilton's Landscape Park

41 The Leasowes, Worcestershire: Engraving by D. Jenkins from *The Modern Universal British Traveller*, 1779

42   Claremont, Surrey: Engraving by W. Watts after Geo. Barrett, R.A., 1779. *Surrey County Library*

43   Claremont, Surrey: A View of the Lake

44   Claremont, Surrey: The House and Park, both by 'Capability' Brown. From an engraving of 1842. *Surrey County Library*

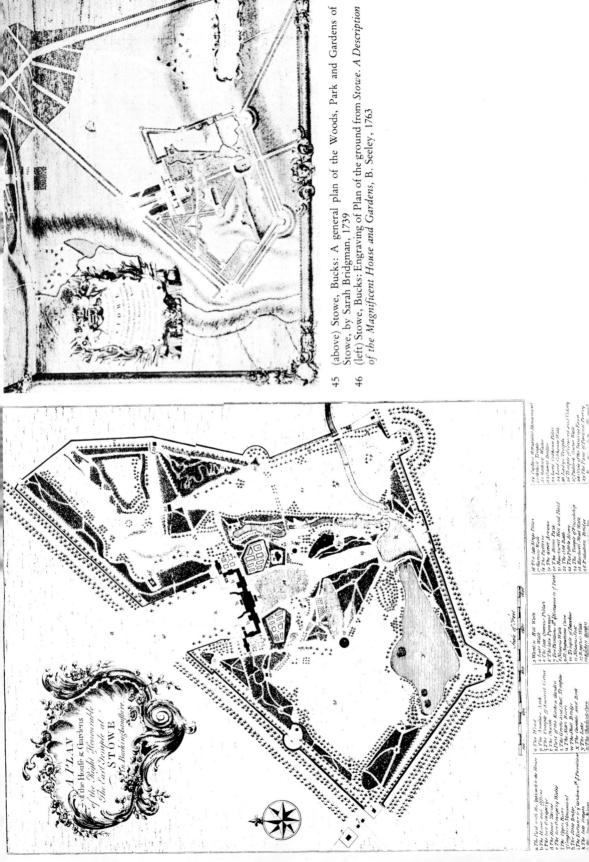

45 (above) Stowe, Bucks: A general plan of the Woods, Park and Gardens of Stowe, by Sarah Bridgman, 1739

46 (left) Stowe, Bucks: Engraving of Plan of the ground from *Stowe. A Description of the Magnificent House and Gardens*, B. Seeley, 1763

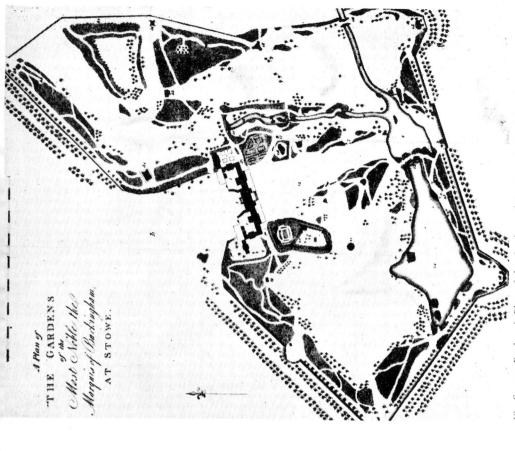

47 Stowe, Bucks: Engraving of Garden Temples and the Shell Bridge, after William Kent

48 Stowe, Bucks: A Plan of the Gardens of the Most Noble Marquis of Buckingham at Stowe, 1777

49 Stowe, Bucks: View of the Grecian Valley from Grenville Column. Drawing by J.B. Chatelain, 1752

50 Stowe, Bucks: View of Alder River from Grotto. Drawing by J.B. Chatelain, 1752

51　Nuneham, Oxfordshire: View of Lord Harcourt's Flower Garden. Engraved by W. Watts, after Paul Sandby, 1777

52　Nuneham, Oxfordshire: View of the Flower Garden at Nuneham. Engraved by W. Watts, after Paul Sandby, 1777

53　Nuneham, Oxfordshire: View of House by Boydell, from *The River Thames. An History of the Principal Rivers of Great Britain* (1794), I, 190

54　Woburn Abbey, Bedfordshire: The Menagerie. Lithograph by F. Ross from *Hortus Woburnensis*, a descriptive catalogue, by James Forbes, 1833

Bowood, Wiltshire: The Cascade made for the Marquis of Lansdowne by Charles Hamilton, after a painting by Gaspar Poussin. *Country Life*

56   Wilton House, Wiltshire: 'The Genius of the Place'